OBSESSIONAL NEUROSES

Developmental Psychopathology

OBSESSIONAL NEUROSES

Developmental Psychopathology

HUMBERTO NAGERA, M.D.

Professor of Psychiatry and Chief of the Youth Service,
University of Michigan

Training Analyst, The Michigan Psychoanalytic Institute

JASON ARONSON, INC.
NEW YORK

ISBN: 0-87668-271-9

Library of Congress Catalog Number: 76-229

typeset by Jeanne Lombardi
New York, N.Y.

Manufactured in the United States of America

to Anna Freud
on the occasion of her eightieth birthday

Series Introduction

The obsessional syndrome has long been of great interest and importance to psychoanalysts. Freud's case study of the Rat Man provided a definitive contribution not only to the understanding of this common clinical problem but also to basic psychoanalytic metapsychology and clinical practice. While the field has seen a number of isolated studies of this entity, it is Humberto Nagera's achievement to have written a careful and detailed clinical-theoretical study of the obsessional neurosis, providing the reader an integrated view long overdue.

This work, the second contribution by Dr. Nagera to this series, stands firmly rooted in the history of classical psychoanalysis while contributing to its most promising future.

Robert Langs, M.D.

Foreword

by ANNA FREUD

The motivation for this elaborate and painstaking piece of work is revealed clearly in the quotation from Freud which initiates it. Humberto Nagera shares Freud's belief that the obsessional neurosis is the most rewarding subject of analytic research, no other mental phenomenon displaying with equal clarity the human quandary of relentless and unceasing battles between innate impulses and acquired moral demands.

In the main part of his book, the author traces Freud's insights into the subject as they advanced and broadened out from their first tentative beginnings in 1895 to some final pronouncements in 1939. He orders these formulations under meaningful headings which range from merely terminological and chronological concerns to the dynamic contributions made to the symptomatology by processes in id, ego and superego.

From this invaluable guide for study, which no average reader could provide for himself, he proceeds with similar thoroughness to the statements made by Freud's coworkers and immediate followers, giving preference among them to two notable teachers and chroniclers of psychoanalysis: Hermann Nunberg and Otto Fenichel. Nevertheless, in regard to these as well as to many of the other clinical and theoretical contributors, he deplores the scarcity of original findings and characterizes the main bulk of publications after Freud as merely amplifying and corroborating.

In his last chapters, Nagera enumerates the directions in which he feels the study of obsessional phenomena may yield further profit. He notes among these clearer distinctions (1) between transient obsessional symptoms as they arise during the ongoing conflicts of the anal-sadistic stage and the obsessional neurosis proper, caused by later regression to that level; (2) between the consequences of obsessionality for normal or abnormal character formation; (3) between obsessive characters on the one hand and obsessive pathology on the other hand; and (4) between the harm done to a functioning personality by hysterical interferences and that done by obsessional interferences. Finally, and most important, he advocates a developmental approach to the etiological problems of the obsessional neurosis—that is, one in which not only a fixation point on the anal-sadistic level is considered of major importance, but one in which the contributions from all, earlier or later, developmental phases are given their due.

It is in this respect especially that the author's dealings with the problems of the obsessional neurosis constitute a welcome continuation of his earlier explorations of developmental disturbances and developmental conflicts as the possible forerunners of true neurotic conflicts, i.e., a continuation of his efforts to create a developmental psychology which encompasses the normal and abnormal problems of all stages of human growth.

Contents

Chapter 3

OBSESSIONAL NEUROSIS AS A FACADE   125

Chapter 4

OBSESSIONAL CHARACTERS AND OBSESSIONAL
NEUROSES   137

Chapter 5

Chapter 6

COMPARING OBSESSIONAL AND HYSTERICAL
PERSONALITIES   191

Chapter 7

A DEVELOPMENTAL APPROACH   197

Chapter 8

GENERAL AND DIAGNOSTIC CONSIDERATIONS   207

Obsessional Neurosis is unquestionably the most interesting and repaying subject of analytic research. But as a problem it has not yet been mastered.

—Sigmund Freud,
Inhibitions, Symptoms and Anxiety.

Preface

We have followed Tyson and Strachey's "A Chronological Hand-List of Freud's Works" as it appeared in the *International Journal of Psycho-Analysis,* Vol. 37, 1956. This list is the one used in the Standard Edition of *The Complete Works of Sigmund Freud.*

Occasionally, for example in chapters 1 and 2, we have made use of square brackets in quotations in order to complement, to clarify, or to put them in their proper context.

In regard to Freud's formulations in obsessional neurosis, as well as to those of other authors, we have not included any clinical examples. We have concentrated on the theoretical conclusions drawn from their study insofar as they contribute to a coherent and comprehensive picture of this particular nosological entity.

In the revision of Freud's concepts, we have left out the relation between obsessions, compulsions, and phobias, because phobias are the object of a study in another project in the Clinical Concept Research Group.

We are grateful to Mrs. M. Cowan for her enthusiasm, devotion and invaluable secretarial help. The same applies to Mrs. B. Houston.

Finally we have a special debt of gratitude to Miss Anna Freud for her many valuable suggestions in relation to content and style.

This study has been partly supported by grant MH-05683 from the National Institute of Mental Health, Bethesda, Maryland, U.S.A.

It was part of the research program of the Clinical Concept Research Group at the Hampstead Child Therapy Clinic and Course, a research group of which I was chairman. Thus, for the first manuscript of this book I gratefully acknowledge the collaboration of Mrs. M. Burgner and the Clinical Concept Research Group of the Hampstead Child Therapy Clinic and Course. I am, nevertheless, totally responsible for that first manuscript and for the final form of the book, which I have completed while a staff member of the Department of Psychiatry at the University of Michigan.

Chapter 1

Freud's Formulations on
Obsessional Neurosis

The Term *Obsessional Neurosis*

According to Strachey, in his footnote to Freud's "Obsessive Actions and Religious Practices" (1907b, p. 117), Loewenfeld (1904) attributes the origin of the concept and the term *obsessional neurosis* to Freud himself. Freud's first published use of it seems to have been in "On the Grounds for Detaching a Particular Syndrome from Neurasthenia under the Description 'Anxiety Neurosis'" (1895b). The term *obsessional idea* or *obsession* is attributed by Loewenfeld to Krafft-Ebbing, who introduced it in 1897.

Onset

In pointing to the ages at which the different forms of psychopathology are to be observed, Freud stated that the first manifestations of obsessional neurosis usually appear between the ages of six and eight. While hysterical forms of illness are observed in earliest childhood, obsessional neurosis generally shows its first symptoms in the second period of childhood, that is, between six and eight. The other two major psychoneuroses—paranoia and dementia praecox—which he brought together under the heading of paraphrenia, do not appear until later, that is, after puberty and during adult life (1913i, p. 318). It is of interest to refer here to a passage quoted by Jones in his biography of Freud which appeared in the minutes of the Vienna Psychoanalytic Society of 17 November 1909. Freud discusses there the fact that all severe neuroses have a prototype in childhood. According to him this is quite evident in the obsessional neurotics: "This neurosis is almost mono-symptomatically concentrated on one point at the age of six to eight [presumably in the conflicts around masturbation], and is already completely formed " (Jones, 1955, p. 493).

Seventeen years later, in *Inhibitions, Symptoms and Anxiety* (1962d, p. 116) Freud made a statement that seems complementary to the previous one considering that during the latency period the main conflictual task is the fending off of the temptation to masturbate. This struggle produces symptoms which appear typically in different individuals and which have the character generally speaking of a ceremonial. . . . Thus they already exhibit the features which emerge so disastrously if a serious illness follows. They tend to become attached to activities (which would later be carried out almost automatically) such as going to sleep, washing, dressing and walking about. They tend also to repetition and waste of time. He did not feel that the reasons for this were clear, but that the sublimation of anal-erotic components played an unmistakable role in it.

Similar passages are to be found in *Inhibitions, Symptoms and Anxiety* (1962d), where he specifically adds that the phallic-oedipal phase must have been reached and that what is fended off are the trends of the Oedipus complex. Thus he said: ". . . by the time an obsessional neurosis is entered upon, the phallic stage has already been reached." He reiterated too that the onset of obsessional neurosis belongs to a later time of life than that of hysteria, that is to the second period of childhood after the latency period has set in (1962d, p. 114). He added that perhaps in obsessional cases more than in normal or hysterical ones we can recognize most clearly the motive force of defense as being the castration complex, and again what is being fended off can be identified as the trends of the Oedipus complex (1962d, p. 114). Since the phallic-oedipal stage is assumed to be reached somewhere between three and five years of age it follows that obsessional neurosis proper (to be distinguished from other obsessional "manifestations" that may occur earlier) can only develop at a somewhat later stage.

In "The Disposition to Obsessional Neurosis" (1913i) Freud

distinguishes between two types of development of obsessional neurosis. The first, after its onset at an early age, runs a chronic course "with exacerbations of a more or less striking kind." In these cases "once the sexual organization which contains the disposition to obsessional neurosis is established [the anal-sadistic stage] it is never afterwards completely surmounted. . . ." In the second type development proceeds to a higher stage, from which a regressive move takes place a a later time (1913i, p. 322). The first explicit link between anal erotism and obsessional neuroses also appears in this paper.

Types of Obsessional Neurosis

In his paper "Further Remarks on the Neuropsychoses of Defence" (1896b) Freud describes three main forms or types of obsessional neurosis (p. 170). In schematic form they appear as follows:

1. Obsessional Ideas
2. Obsessional Affects:
    —self-reproaches
    —shame
    —hypochondriacal anxiety
    —social anxiety
    —delusions of being noticed
    —fear of temptation, etc.
3. Obsessional Actions:
    —penitential ceremonies:
        —burdensome ceremonials
        —observations of numbers, etc.
    —precautionary measures:
        —all sorts of phobias
        —pedantry
        —superstition
        —overconscientiousness
    —fear of betrayal:
        —collecting scraps of paper
        —seclusiveness
    —measures ensuring numbing of the mind.
        —dipsomania, etc.

1. Obsessional ideas. Obsessional ideas characterize the first form. In this type, according to Freud, what forces its way into consciousness is the memory of an act that should involve self-reproach, but where the self-reproachful affect is kept out of consciousness, ". . . the content engages the patient's attention and, as an affect, he merely feels an indefinite unpleasure, whereas the only affect which would be suitable to the obsessional idea will be one of self-reproach" (1896b, p. 170). Freud added that obsessional ideas were invariably transformed self-reproaches which re-emerge from repression. They always relate to some sexual act that was performed with pleasure in childhood (1896b, p. 269). This was the phase of the sexual-seduction theory of hysteria and obsessional neuroses that was soon to be abandoned. As to the distortion that takes place in this condition, he said that the content of the obsessional thought is distorted in two ways in relation to the obsessional act of childhood. "First, something sexual is replaced by something analogous to it that is not sexual" (1896b, 170). These distortions are the result of the tendency to repress, still in force, which he ascribes to the "ego." Some thirteen years later in "Notes Upon a Case of Obsessional Neurosis" (1909d) Freud reconsidered some of the previous statements, introducing some important reformulations and amplifications. Thus, he remarks on how in 1896 he defined obsessional ideas as transformed self-reproaches which have reemerged from repression, always related to some sexual act performed with pleasure in childhood. This definition now seemed to him open to criticism upon formal grounds, though its component elements were still unobjectable. This change was the result of his aiming too much at unification and, as he said, of taking as a model the practice of obsessional neurotics themselves, when, with their characteristic liking for indeterminateness, they heaped together under the name *obsessional ideas* the most heterogeneous psychical structures. He thought it would be more correct to speak of "obsessive thinking", making clear that obsessional structures can correspond to every sort of psychical act, i.e., wishes, temptations, impulses, reflections, doubts, commands, or prohibitions. He added that patients tend to tone down such distinctions and to regard what remains of these psychical acts (after they have been deprived of their affective index) simply as "obsessional ideas." . . . He remarked on how the phenomenology of obsessional thinking has not had sufficient attention paid to it. Thus, he pointed out how during the secondary defensive struggle (which the patient carries on against the "obsessional ideas" that have forced their way into his consciousness) psychical structures make their appearance which deserve to be given a special name. . . . obsessional thoughts, but, as it were, hybrids between the two species of thinking. They accept certain of the premises of the obsession they are combating, and thus, though using the weapons of reason, are established upon a basis of pathological thought. He thought that such structures deserved to be given the name *deliria* (1909d, p. 221).

In the same paper (1909d) he further explained that the patients themselves may not always know the wording of their obsessional ideas. Thus he says that during analysis "the patient, who has hitherto turned his eyes away in terror from his own pathological productions, begins to attend to them and obtains a clearer and more detailed view of them." In a footnote to the above he adds: "Some patients carry the diversion of their attention to such lengths that they are totally unable to give the content of an obsessional idea or to describe an obsessional act though they have performed it over and over again" (1909d, p. 223; cf. also 1909b, p. 124).

In relation to "obsessional ideas" he explained that when a number of them succeed one another they are one and the same, though the wording may be different. This is accounted for as the return in distorted form of the original "obsessional idea" that was rejected. When we have at great pains elucidated an unintelligible obsessional idea, it often happens that the patient informs us that just such a notion, wish, or temptation as the one we have constructed did in fact make its appearance on one occasion before the obsessional idea had arisen, [the present distorted one], but that it did not persist" (1909d, 10:224).

2. Obsessional affects. Obsessional affects characterize the second type of obsessional neurosis. In this type what has forced its way into consciousness "is not the repessed mnemic content but the likewise repressed self-reproach" (1896b, p. 171). He considered that this affect of self-reproach could, by means of some mental additions, be transformed into any other type of unpleasurable affect. If this happened there was no longer anything to prevent the submitted affect from becoming conscious:

> Thus *self-reproach* (for having carried out the sexual act in childhood) can easily turn into *shame* (in case someone else should find out about it), into *hypochondriacal anxiety* (fear of the physical injuries resulting from the act involving the self-reproach), into *religious anxiety,* into *delusions of being noticed* (fear of betraying the act to other people), or into *fear of temptation* (a justified mistrust of one's own moral powers of resistance), and so on. In addition, the mnemic content of the act involving self-reproach may be represented in consciousness as well, or it may remain completely in the background—which makes diagnosis much more difficult [1896b, p. 171].

3. Obsessional acts. Obsessional acts constitute the third form or type of obsessional neurosis. A most important characteristic of these obsessional actions is that they are never primary. "They never contain anything but a defence—never an aggression" (1896b, p. 172).

These obsessional actions are rather in the nature of *"protective measures."* In the first two forms of obsessional neurosis (obsessional ideas and obsessional affects) the symptoms are compromise symptoms due to the return of the repressed after the failure of the original defense organization. At this point in the development of an obsessional neurosis a new set of symptoms is constructed, consisting of "actions," "protective measures" against the obsessional ideas and affects. They are a sort of *"secondary defense"against the derivatives of the initially repressed memory.*

Freud explained that if these aids in the defensive struggle are truly successful in once more repressing the symptoms of the return of the repressed (which have forced themselves on the ego), "then the obsession is transferred to the protective measures themselves and creates a third form of 'obsessional neurosis'—obsessional actions" (1896b, p. 172). He continued:

> Secondary defence against the obsessional ideas may be effected by a forcible diversion onto other thoughts with a content as

contrary as possible. This is why *obsessional brooding*, if it succeeds, regularly deals with abstract and *suprasensual* things; because the ideas that have been repressed are always concerned with *sensuality*. Or else the patient tries to make himself master of each of his obsessional ideas singly by logical work and by having recourse to his conscious memories. This leads to *obsessional thinking*, to *a compulsion to test things* and to *doubting mania*. Secondary defence against obsessional *affects* leads to a still wider set of protective measures which are capable of being transformed into obsessional acts. These may be grouped according to their purpose: *penitential* measures (burdensome ceremonials, the observation of numbers), *precautionary* measures (all sorts of phobias, superstition, pedantry, increase of the primary symptom of conscientiousness), measures to do with *fear of betrayal* (collecting scraps of paper, seclusiveness), or to ensure *numbing* [of the mind] (dypsomania). Among these obsessional acts and obsessional impulses, phobias, since they circumscribe the patient's existence, play the greatest part [1896b, p. 173]

In "Obsessive Actions and Religious Practices" (1907b) he stated that we ought not to expect to find sharp distinctions between "ceremonials" and "obsessive actions" since as a rule obsessive actions have grown out of ceremonials. Beyond these two, prohibitions and hindrances (abulias) make up the content of the disorder; they, in fact, only continue the work of the obsessive actions, "inasmuch as some things are completely forbidden to the patient and others only allowed subject to his following a prescribed ceremonial" (1907b, p. 118ff).

In "Notes Upon a Case of Obsessional Neurosis" (1909d)—he described certain forms of compulsive acts that occur, in two successive steps, of which the second neutralises the first, as typical occurrences in the obsessional neurosis. "The patient's consciousness naturally misunderstands them and puts forward a set of secondary motives to account for them—*rationalises* them, in short. But their true significance lies in their being a representation of a conflict between two opposing impulses of approximately equal strength: and hitherto I have invariably found that this opposition has been one between love and hate" (p. 192).

Later on in the same paper he points out how the obsessional acts tend to approximate more and more to infantile sexual acts of a masturbatory character, a situation that becomes more evident the longer the disorder lasts (p. 244).

Similarly, in *Totem and Taboo* (1912x): "It is possible, however, to describe the course of development of obsessive acts: We can show how they begin by being as remote as possible from anything sexual— magical defences against evil wishes—and how they end by being substitutes for the forbidden sexual act and the closest possible imitations of it" (p.88).

Finally, Freud in the same work made it quite clear that one can frequently observe either the one type or the other in obsessional neuroses or several different combinations of them, as well as possible alternations, in the same case, from the one type to the others.

There are cases in which one can observe how the obsession is transferred from the idea or from the affect onto the protective measure; others in which the obsession oscillates periodically between the symptom of the return of the repressed and the symptom of the secondary defence; and yet other cases in which no obsessional idea is constructed at all but, instead, the repressed memory is at once represented by what is apparently a primary measure of defence. Here we reach at one bound the stage which elsewhere only completes the course run by the obsessional neurosis after the defensive struggle has taken place. Severe cases of this disorder end in the ceremonial actions becoming fixated, or in a general state of doubting mania, or in a life of eccentricity conditioned by phobias. [p. 173ff.]

Similarly in the *Introductory Lectures on Psycho-Analysis* (1916x):

In different forms and cases of obsessional neurosis the pathological ideas, impulses and actions are not combined in equal proportions: it is the rule, rather that one or other of these factors dominates the picture and gives its name to the illness but the common element in all these forms is sufficiently unmistakable [p. 259].

Etiological Considerations

For some time in the nineties Freud postulated that seductive sexual experiences in childhood were at the basis of hysteria and obsessional neurosis (a passive experience of seduction for hysteria, an active one for obsessional neurosis). By September 1897, in a letter to Fliess (No. 69) he was already doubtful about this and had started to recognize the part played by fantasy in mental life. According to Strachey (Freud, 1896b, p. 160, ed.'s note), it was not until 1906 that Freud gave public expression to his changed opinions.

Thus, in "Heredity and the Aetiology of the Neurosis (*Zwangsneurose*) arises from a specific cause analogous to that of hysteria:

> Here too we find a precocious sexual event, occurring before puberty, the memory of which becomes active during or after that period; and the same remarks and arguments which I put forward in connection with hysteria will apply to my observations of the other neurosis. . . . There is only one difference which seems capital. At the basis of the aetiology of hysteria we found an event of passive sexuality. . . . In obsessional neurosis it is a question, on the other hand, of an event which has given *pleasure,* of an act of aggression inspired by desire (in the case of a boy) or of a participation in sexual relations accompanied by enjoyment (in the case of a little girl). The obsessional ideas, when their intimate meaning has been recognized by analysis, when they have been reduced, as it were, to their simplest expression, are nothing other than *reproaches addressed by the subject to himself on account of this anticipated sexual enjoyment,* but reproaches distorted by an unconscious psychical work of transformation and substitution. [p. 155]

Similarly in his paper "Further Remarks on the Neuro-Psychoses of Defence" (1896b) he stated:

> Sexual experiences of early childhood have the same significance in the aetiology of obsessional neurosis as they have in that of hysteria. Here, however, it is no longer a question of sexual *passivity* [as in hysteria], but of acts of aggression carried out with pleasure and of pleasurable participation in sexual acts—that is to say, of sexual *activity.* The difference in the aetiological circumstances is

bound up with the fact that obsessionaw neurosis shows a visible preference for the male sex. [p. 168]

In the footnote added in 1924 to this paper Freud wrote that at that time he was not yet able

to distinguish between my patients' phantasies about their childhood years and their real recollections. As a result, I attributed to the aetiological factor of seduction a significance and universality which it does not possess. When this error had been overcome, it became possible to obtain an insight into the spontaneous manifestations of the sexuality of children. . . . [p. 168]

He thought that "precocious sexual aggressivity always implies a previous experience of being seduced. . . . The decision as to whether hysteria or obsessional neurosis will rise on the basis of traumas in childhood depends on *chronological* circumstances in the development of the libido" (p. 169).

He summarized his views on the causation of obsessional neurosis at this point in the development of his thought in the following way:

The nature of obsessional neurosis can be expressed in a simple formula. *Obsessional ideas* are invariably transformed *self-reproaches* which have re-emerged from *repression* and which always relate to some sexual act that was performed with pleasure in *childhood.* [p. 169]

He described the typical course taken by an obsessional neurosis as follows:

In a first period—the period of childhood immorality—the events occur which contain the germ of the later neurosis. First of all, in earliest childhood, we have the experiences of sexual seduction that will later on make repression possible; and then come the acts of sexual agression against the other sex, which will later appear in the form of acts involving self-reproach. This period is brought to a close by the advent of sexual "maturation," often itself unduly early. A self-reproach now becomes attached to the memory of these pleasurable actions; and the connection with the initial experience of passivity makes it possible—often only after conscious and remembered efforts—to repress them and to replace them by a *primary symptom of defence.* Conscientiousness, shame and self-distrust are symptoms of this kind, with which the third period begins—the period of *apparent* health, but actually, of unsuccessful defence.

The next period, that of the illness, is characterized by the *return of the repressed memories*—that is, therefore, by the failure of the defence. It is not certain whether the awakening of those memories occurs more often accidentally and spontaneously or as a result of current sexual disturbances, as a kind of by-product of them. The reactivated memories, however, and the self-reproaches formed from them never re-emerge into consciousness unchanged: what become conscious as obsessional ideas and affects, and take the place of the pathogenic memories so far as conscious life is concerned, are structures in the nature of a compromise between the repressed ideas and the repressing ones. [pp. 169-170]

In "Obsessive Actions and Religious Practices" (1907b) the seduction theories have clearly been abandoned by Freud and the emphasis is now on the repression of the instincutal impulses. He says:

A deeper insight into the mechanism of obsessional neurosis is gained if we take into account the primary fact which lies at the bottom of it. This is always the repression of an *instinctual impulse* (a component of the sexual instinct) which was present in the subject's constitution and which was allowed to find expression for a while during his childhood but later succumbed to suppression. In the course of the repression of this instinct a special *conscientious-ness* is created which is directed against the instinct's aims; but this psychical reaction-formation feels insecure and constantly threatened by the instinct which is lurking in the unconscious. The influence of the repressed instinct is felt as a temptation, and during the process of repression itself anxiety is generated, which gains control over the future in the form of *expectant* anxiety. The process of repression which leads to obsessional neurosis must be considered as one which is only partly successful and which increasingly threatens to fail. It may thus be compared to an unending conflict; fresh psychical efforts are continually required to counter-balance the forward pressure of the instinct. [1907b, p. 124]

In the *Introductory Lectures* (1916x) he refers to the problem of causality of the neurosis in the following terms: "For you must know that the same factors always come into operation in the causation and mechanism of every possible form of neurosis; but the chief importance in the construction of the symptoms falls now upon one and now upon another of these factors (1916x, p. 381).

As we have seen the causality of obsessional neurosis is no simple matter. Freud pointed to many of the factors that combine to produce this outcome, as for example the fact that it originates, as hysteria does, in "the necessity of fending off the libidinal demands of the Oedipus complex" (1962d, p. 113), coupled with the factor of regression to the fixation at the anal-sadistic stage, the ego—superego reaction to this regression, and to the defusion thus brought about, etc. etc. (all these aspects are discussed below). At the same time he was far from satisfied, and pointed to the serious gaps in our knowledge in respect to the developmental disposition to neurosis and especially in respect to the ego side of all these problems. This will be further discussed in a later chapter.

Anal Phase and Obsessional Neuroses

The first written explicit link between anal erotism and obsessional neurosis appears in "The Disposition to Obsessional Neurosis" (1913i), though as Strachey points out (1908b, p. 168), the connection between money and miserliness with feces dates from as far back as 1897 (1950a, No. 79).

Yet, in his paper on "Character and Anal Erotism" (1908b), Freud says:

Among those whom we try to help by our psychoanalytic efforts we often come across a type of person who is marked by the possession of a certain set of character-traits, while at the same time our attention is drawn to the behaviour in his childhood of one of his bodily functions and the organ concerned in it. . . . [Such persons] are noteworthy for a regular combination of the three following characteristics. They are especially *orderly, parsimonious* and *obstinate.* [p. 169] childhood of one of his bodily functions and the organ concerned in it. . . . [Such persons] are noteworthy for a regular combination of the three following characteristics. They are especially *orderly, parsimonious* and *obstinate.* [p. 169]

Similarly, in "Notes Upon a Case of Obsessional Neurosis" (1909d) he refers "to the important part played by the sadistic instinctual components in the genesis of obsessional neurosis" (pp. 240, 245).

As mentioned above it was in "The Disposition to Obsessional Neurosis" (1913i) that Freud clearly established for the first time in his written work the link between obsessional neurosis and as he put it at that time the anal-erotic and sadistic impulses. It was this link that forced on him the need to interpolate in his theory of libidinal development a new phase not so far taken into account. Thus he says:

And now we see the need for yet another stage to be inserted before the final shape is reached—a stage in which the component instincts have already come together for the choice of an object and that is already something extraneous in contrast to the subject's own self, but in which *the primacy of the genital zones has not yet been established.* On the contrary, the component instincts which dominate this pregenital organization of sexual life are the anal-erotic and sadistic ones. [1913, p. 321]

A few lines later he continues:

The extraordinary part played by impulses of hatred and anal erotism in the symptomatology of obsessional neurosis has already struck many observers and has recently been emphasized with particular clarity by Ernest Jones (1913). This follows directly from our hypothesis if we suppose that in that neurosis the component instincts in question have once more taken over the representation of the genital instincts, whose fore-runners they were in the process of development. [p. 321]

The Role of the Oedipus Complex in Obsessional Neuroses

The essential role of the Oedipus complex in the development of the various neuroses is a well-established fact in psychoanalysis. Obsessional neuroses are in no way an exception to this rule. Thus Freud said:

> It is perhaps in obsessional cases more than in normal or hysterical ones that we can most clearly recognize that the motive force of defence is the castration complex and that what is being fended off are the trends of the Oedipus complex. We are at present dealing with the beginning of the latency period, a period which is characterized by the dissolution of the Oedipus complex, the creation or consolidation of the super-ego and the erection of ethical and aesthetic barriers in the ego. In obsessional neuroses these processes are carried further than is normal. [1962d, p. 114]

And: "obsessional neuroses originates, no doubt, from the same situation as hysteria, namely the necessity of fending off the libidinal demands of the Oedipus complex" (1962d, p. 113).

Since both entities have this same conflict in common, the differences between these two disturbances are partly to be explained by the regressive move of the drive organization to different fixation points. (See also in the present work the next section, "Regression in Obsessional Neurosis," and the later section "Obsessional Neurosis and Hysteria").

Regression in Obsessional Neuroses

The all-important question of the regressive move in obsessional neurosis is perhaps best described by Freud in the *Introductory Lectures* (1916-17), though references to this problem are to be found in many of his writings:

> In obsessional neurosis, on the contrary, it is the regression of the libido to the preliminary stage of the sadistic-anal organization that is the most striking fact and the one which is decisive for what is manifested in symptoms. The love-impulse is obliged, when this has happened, to disguise itself as a sadistic impulse. The obsessional idea "I should like to kill you," when it has been freed from certain additions which are not a matter of chance but are indispensable,

means at bottom nothing other than "I should like to enjoy you in love." If you consider further that there has been a simultaneous regression in regard to the object, so that these impulses apply only to those who are nearest and dearest to the patient, you can form some idea of the horror which these obsessions arouse in him and at the same time of the alien appearance which they present to his conscious perception. [1916x, pp. 343-344]

While describing how the beginning of the latency period is characterized by the dissolution of the Oedipus complex, the consolidation of the super-ego and the erection of ethical and aesthetical barriers, Freud remarked that in obsessional neuroses all these processes are exaggerated:

In obsessional neuroses these procedures are carried further than is normal. In addition to the destruction of the Oedipus complex, a regressive degradation of the libido takes place, the super-ego becomes exceptionally severe and unkind, and the ego, in obedience to the super-ego, produces strong reaction-formations in the shape of conscientiousness, pity and cleanliness. Implacable, though not always on that account successful, severity is shown in condemning the temptation to continue early infantile masturbation, which now attaches itself to regressive (sadistic-anal) ideas but which nevertheless represents the unsubjugated part of the phallic organization. There is an inherent contradiction about this state of affairs, in which, precisely in the interests of masculinity (that is to say, from fear of castration), every activity belonging to masculinity is stopped. But here, too, obsessional neurosis is only overdoing the normal method of getting rid of the Oedipus complex. [1925d, pp. 114-115]

Similarly: "On . . . obsessional neurotics we can observe the result of a regressive debasement of the genital organization. This is expressed in the fact that every phantasy originally conceived on the genital level is transposed to the anal level—the penis being replaced by the fecal mass and the vagina by the rectum" (1917c, p. 127).

It is through the regression to the anal-sadistic fixation and the instinctual defusion that goes with it that some of the specific

characteristics of the obsessional neurosis can be more readily
understood, such as its strong sadistic aspects, the severity of the
superego, etc. In *The Ego and the Id* (1923b) he said:

> . . . we come to understand that instinctual defusion and the
> marked emergence of the death instinct call for particular
> consideration among the effects of some severe neuroses—for
> instance, the obsessional neuroses. Making a swift generalization,
> we might conjecture that the essence of a regression of libido (e.g.
> from the genital to the sadistic-anal phase) lies in a defusion of
> instincts, just as, conversely, the advance from the earlier phase to
> the definitive genital one would be conditioned by an accession of
> erotic components. The question also arises whether ordinary
> ambivalence, which is so often unusually strong in the constitutional
> disposition to neurosis, should not be regarded as the product of a
> defusion; ambivalence, however, is such a fundamental phenomen-
> on that it more probably represents an instinctual fusion that has
> not been completed. [p. 42]

And in the same work: "In obsessional neurosis it has become
possible, through a regression to the pregenital organization, for the
love-impulses to transform themselves into impulses of aggression
against the object. Here again the instinct of destruction has been set
free and it seeks to destroy the object, or at least it appears to have that
intention" (p. 53). And: "The defusion of love [in obsessional neuroses]
into aggressiveness has not been effected by the work of the ego, but is
the result of a regression which has come about in the id" (p.55).

Referring to the advent of puberty and its impact on the obsessional
neurosis Freud made the following important statement: "Not only
will the early aggressive impulses be re-awakened; but a greater or
lesser proportion of the new libidinal impulses—in bad cases the whole
of them—will have to follow the course prescribed for them by
regression and will emerge as aggressive and destructive tendencies"
(1926d, p. 116).

He explained that though obsessional neurosis and hysteria
originate out of the necessity of fending off the demands of the Oedipus
complex they are subsequently directed along different lines largely
because of the regression and its nature. He thought that this was due

either to a constitutional factor or perhaps to a time factor. Thus he said of the constitutional factor:

> The genital organization of the libido turns out to be feeble and insufficiently resistant, so that when the ego begins its defensive efforts the first thing it succeeds in doing is to throw back the genital organization (of the phallic phase), in whole or in part, to the earlier sadistic-anal level. This fact of regression is decisive for all that follows.
>
> Another possibility has to be considered. Perhaps regression is the result not of a constitutional factor but of a time-factor. It may be that regression is rendered possible not because the genital organization of the libido is too feeble but because the opposition of the ego begins too early, while the sadistic phase is at its height. I am not prepared to express a definite opinion on this point, but I may say that analytic observation does not speak in favor of such an assumption. It shows rather that, by the time an obsessional neurosis is entered upon, the phallic state has already been reached. Moreover, the onset of this neurosis belongs to a later time of life than that of hysteria—to the second period of childhood, after the latency period has set in. [1962d, pp. 113-114]

The same question of the time factor was perhaps better explained in a much earlier work of 1913 where it was considered a possible factor *in the disposition* to the illness. He said: "I suggest the possibility that a chronological outstripping of libidinal development by ego development should be included in the disposition to obsessional neurosis" (1913i, p. 325).

Aggression in Obsessional Neuroses

The all-important role of the aggressive drive and the conflicts around aggression in obsessional neurotics was quite clearly established very early in Freud's works. As early as 1897 he said in a Letter to Fliess: (1950a, draft N): "Hostile impulses against parents (a wish that they should die) are also an integral constituent of neuroses. They come to light consciously as obsessional ideas." In any case, the role of aggression is clearly to be seen more than a decade before aggression, as the form of expression of the death instinct, came to represent one of the two essential sets of instincts in psychoanalytic theory as postulated in 1920. Up to that point, aggressive impulses were considered by Freud to be one of the many component instincts of the sexual drive. It is indeed striking to notice how near to the 1920 formulations on instinct theory (in *Beyond the Pleasure Principle*) are many of his formulations in 1909d ("Notes upon a case of Obsessional Neurosis"): "If we consider a number of analyses of obsessional neurotics we shall find it impossible to escape the impression that a relation between love and hatred . . . is among the most frequent, the most marked, and probably, therefore, the most important characteristic of obsessional neurosis" (p. 239).

He considered he knew too little about the nature of love to be able to arrive at any definite conclusion and in a tentative way continued:

We may suppose, then, that in the cases of unconscious hatred with which we are concerned the sadistic components of love have, from constitutional causes, been exceptionally strongly developed, and have consequently undergone a premature and all too thorough repression, and that the neurotic phenomena we have observed arise on the one hand from conscious feelings of affection which have become exaggerated as a reaction, and on the other hand from sadism perisisting in the unconscious in the form of hatred. [p. 240]

In *Totem and Taboo* (1912x) he stated:

An obsessional neurotic may be weighed down by a sense of guilt that would be appropriate in a mass-murderer, while in fact, from his childhood onwards, he has behaved to his fellow-men as the most considerate and scrupulous member of society. Nevertheless, his sense of guilt has a justification: it is founded on the intense and frequent death-wishes against his fellows which are unconsciously at work in him. It has a justification if what we take into account are unconscious thoughts and not intentional deeds. . . . Whenever I have succeeded in penetrating the mystery, I have found that the expected disaster was death. [p. 87]

And in "The Disposition to Obsessional Neuroses" (1913i) he said:

> The extraordinary part played by impulses of hatred and anal erotism in the symptomatology of obsessional neurosis has already struck many observers and has recently been emphasized with particular clarity by Ernest Jones. This follows directly from our hypothesis if we suppose that in that neurosis the component instincts in question have once more taken over the representation of the genital instincts, whose forerunners they were in the process of development. [p. 321]

In his paper "Repression" (1915d), he explained how in obsessional neurosis there may be at first some doubt with regard to "the instinctual representative that is subjected to repression—whether it is a libidinal or hostile trend. This uncertainty arises because obsessional neurosis has as its basis a regression owing to which a sadistic trend has been substituted for an affectionate one" (p. 156).

We have referred in the section "Regression in Obsessional Neurosis" to the fact that the regressive process leads to defusion. In this way much of the libidinal impulses following the regressive path will emerge as aggressive and destructive tendencies with an over-all increase in aggressiveness and in the strength of the anal-sadistic impulses. This is perhaps better expressed in the following quotation that we repeat here: "In obsessional neurosis it has become possible, through a regression to the pre-genital organization, for the love impulses to transform themselves into impulses of aggression against the object. Here again the instinct of destruction has been set free and it seeks to destroy the object, or at least it appears to have that intention" (1923b, p. 53).

In the *Introductory Lectures on Psycho-Analysis* (1916x) he made it clear that the frightening murderous fantasies are never translated into action in obsessional neurosis:

> The impulses which the patient is aware of in himself may also make a childish and senseless impression, but as a rule they have a content of the most frightful kind, tempting him, for instance, to commit serious crimes, so that he not merely disavows them as alien to himself, but flies from them in horror and protects himself from

carrying them out by prohibitions, renunciations and restrictions upon his freedom. At the same time, these impulses never—literally never—force their way through to performance; the outcome lies always in victory for the flight and the precautions. [p. 258]

In "Notes Upon a Case of Obsessional Neurosis" (1909d) he remarked on the true significance of the compulsive acts in obsessional neuroses lying ". . . in their being a representation of a conflict between two opposing impulses of approximately equal strength: and hitherto I have invariably found that this opposition has been one between love and hate" (p. 192). And later on: ". . . like other obsessional neurotics, our patient was compelled to overestimate the effects of his hostile feelings upon the external world, because a large part of their internal mental effects escaped his conscious knowledge. His love—or rather his hatred—was in truth overpowering; it was precisely they that created the obsessional thoughts, of which he could not understand the origin and against which he strove in vain to defend himself" (pp. 234-235).

Freud pointed out that very frequently the actual wording or true content of the aggressive fantasy only penetrates consciousness in the form of a rather distorted, vague or indiscriminate notion so as to be largely unrecognizable by the ego. He further stated that:

Even where repression has not encroached upon the content of the aggressive impulse it has certainly got rid of its accompanying affective character. As a result, the aggressiveness appears to the ego not to be an impulsion but, as the patients themselves say, merely a "thought" which awakens no feeling. [1926d, p. 117]

The frequent taboo against touching in this form of illness is explained as follows: "Since obsessional neurosis begins by persecuting erotic touching and then, after regression has taken place, goes on to persecute touching in the guise of aggressiveness, it follows that nothing is so strongly proscribed in that illness as touching nor so well suited to become the central point of a system of prohibitions." And: ". . . the answer is that touching and physical contact are the immediate aim of the aggressive as well as the loving object-cathexes" (1926d, p.122).

Characteristics and Clinical Picture

The clinical picture presented by obsessional neurotics will show specific variations in different cases. Generally speaking one or another of the forms described under "Types of Obsessional Neurosis" will be central in the clinical picture, though not infrequently what will be observed is a combination of the different types in varying proportions. Thus in some patients "obsessional affects" or "obsessional or compulsive acts" are to be observed while in still another group combinations of all the above forms exist. There is in this illness a very wide range of clinical variations that are nevertheless within the frame of the peculiarities of the obsessional processes.

Furthermore, there are a number of other traits to be found in general in every obsessional neurosis, that characterize and complete, in different proportions and combinations, the clincial picture of any given case. There are, for example, a more or less marked tendency to uncertainty and doubting, a strong belief in the omnipotence of thoughts and actions, obsessional thinking, signs of marked ambivalent feelings etc.

Lack of belief in the obsessional thoughts. Etc. One important characteristic of obsessional neurotics had already been described in his paper "Further Remarks on the Neuro-Psychoses of Defence" (1896b) where Freud made it quite clear that neither the "obsessional ideas" nor any of their derivatives met with any belief on the part of the subject that suffered from them. He knew they are not real but his knowledge did not help his suffering condition. As Freud said:

The "obsessional" character of the psychical formations which I have described here has quite generally nothing to do with attaching belief to them. Nor is it to be confused with the factor which is described as the "strength" or "intensity" of an idea. Its essence is rather indissolubility by psychical activity that is capable of being conscious; and this attribute undergoes no change, whether the idea to which the obsession attaches is stronger or weaker, or less or more intensely "illuminated," or "cathected with energy" and so on. The case of this invulnerability of the obsessional idea and its derivatives is however nothing more than its connection with the repressed memory from early childhood. For if we can succeed in making that connection conscious—and psychotherapeutic methods already appear able to do so—the obsession, too, is resolved. [1896b, p. 174]

In the *Introductory Lectures on Psycho-Analysis* (1916x) he repeated:

Obsessional neurosis is shown in the patient's being occupied with thoughts in which he is in fact not interested, in his being aware of impulses in himself which appear very strange to him and in his being led to actions the performance of which gives him no enjoyment, but which it is quite impossible for him to omit. The thoughts (obsessions) may be senseless in themselves, or merely a matter of indifference to the subject; often they are completely silly, and invariably they are the starting-point of a strenuous mental activity, which exhausts the patient and to which he only surrenders himself most unwillingly. He is obliged against his will to brood and speculate as though it were a question of his most important vital problems. . . . [He continued:] Do not suppose, however, that you will help the patient in the least by calling on him . . . to cease to occupy himself with such foolish thoughts and to do something sensible instead of his childish pranks. He would like to do so himself, for he is completely clear in his head, shares your opinion of his obsessional symptoms and even puts it forward to you spontaneously. Only he cannot help himself. [pp. 258-259]

In "Obsessive Actions and Religious Practices" (1907b) Freud comes back to the same question:

Neurotic ceremonials consist in making small adjustments to particular everyday actions, small additions or restrictions or arrangements, which have always to be carried out in the same, or in a methodically varied manner. There activities give the impression of being mere formalities, and they seem quite meaningless to us. Nor do they appear otherwise to the patient himself, yet he is incapable of giving them up, for any deviation from the ceremonial is visited by intolerable anxiety, which obliges him at once to make his omission good. [p. 118]

Anxiety at the interruption of the ritual. In the anxiety provoked by the interruption or even the slightest deviation from the ceremonial we have another important characteristic of obsessional neuroses that helps to establish the amount of psychopathological involvement in any tendency to order, method or meticulosity. Freud said:

Thus in slight cases the ceremonial seems to be no more than an exaggeration of an orderly procedure that is customary and justifiable; but the special consciousness with which it is carried out and the anxiety which follows upon its neglect stamp the ceremonial as a "sacred act." Any interruption of it is for the most part badly tolerated, and the presence of other people during its performance is almost always ruled out.

. . . .We shall not expect to find a sharp distinction between "ceremonials" and "obsessive actions." As a rule obsessive actions have grown out of ceremonials. Besides these two, prohibitions and hindrances (abulias) make up the content of the disorder; these, in fact, only continue the work of the obsessive actions, inasmuch as some things are completely forbidden to the patient and others only allowed subject to his following a prescribed ceremonial.

It is remarkable that both compulsions and prohibitions (having to do something and having *not* to do something) apply in the first instance only to the subject's solitary activities and for a long time leave his social behavior unaffected. Sufferers from this illness are consequently able to treat their affliction as a private matter and keep it concealed for many years. [1907b, pp. 118-119]

Similarly in his "Notes Upon a Case of Obsessional Neurosis" (1909d) he said: "If it happens that a compulsive command cannot be obeyed, the tension becomes intolerable and is perceived by the patient in the form of extreme anxiety" (p. 244).

Knowing and not knowing in obsessional neurosis. One perhaps somewhat strange characteristic of the obsessional neurotic is that he "knows" and "does not know" about some of his symptoms, traumas, etc. at one and the same time. This peculiarity was attributed by Freud to the type of defense mechanisms used in this illness. He said:

It must therefore be admitted that in an obsessional neurosis there are two kinds of knowledge, and it is just as reasonable to hold that the patient knows his traumas as that he does *not* know them. For he knows them in that he has not forgotten them, and he does not know them in that he is unaware of their significance. [1909d, p. 196, n. 1]

Freud frequently pointed out the role that the instinct for knowledge plays in obsessionals. This is no doubt an important characteristic of many obsessionals. He said for example:

In particular we often gain an impression that the instinct for knowledge can actually take the place of sadism in the mechanism of obsessional neurosis. Indeed it is at bottom a sublimated off-shoot of the instinct of mastery exalted into something intellectual, and its repudiation in the form of doubt plays a large part in the picture of obsessional neurosis. [1913i, p. 324]

And earlier on in his paper "Notes Upon a Case of Obsessional Neurosis" (1909d) he had already remarked: "The histories of obsessional patients almost invariably reveal an early development and premature repression of the sexual instinct of looking and knowing . . . " (p. 245). He continued in a footnote to the above: "The very high average of intellectual capacity among obsessional patients is probably also connected with this fact" (p. 245, n. 1).

Thinking in obsessional neurosis. The special quality and the very special role of the thought processes in the obsessional neurosis is a very familiar and well accepted fact.

In his paper "Notes Upon a Case of Obsessional Neurosis" (1909d) Freud stated that when the epistemophilic instinct is preponderant in the constitution of an obsessional patient, brooding becomes the principal symptom of the neurosis. Thought processes themselves become sexualized, for the sexual pleasure which is normally attached to the content of the thought is shifted onto the act of thinking itself, and thus the satisfaction derived from reaching the conclusion of a line of thought is experienced as a *sexual* satisfaction. He continued:

> In the various forms of obsessional neurosis in which the epistemophilic instinct plays a part, its relation to thought-processes makes it particularly well adapted to attract the energy which is vainly endeavouring to make its way forward into action, and divert it into the sphere of thought, where there is a possibility of its obtaining pleasurable satisfaction of another sort. In this way, with the help of the epistemophilic instinct, the substitutive act may in its turn be replaced by preparatory acts of thought. But procrastination in *action* is soon replaced by lingering over *thoughts,* and eventually the whole process, together with all its peculiarities, is transferred into the new sphere. . . . [p. 245]

He further explained that in some obsessionals "by a sort of *regression* preparatory acts become substitutes for the final decision, thinking replaces acting, and, instead of the substitutive act, some thought preliminary to it asserts itself with all the force of compulsion. *According as this regression from acting to thinking is more or less marked, a case of obsessional neurosis will exhibit the characteristics of obsessive thinking* (that is, of obsessional ideas) *or of obsessive acting in the narrower sense of the word"* (p. 244).

We have already referred to the part that obsessional thoughts can play in this illness and especially in some of its clinical forms. This can be repeated here as a contrast to what has been described above in relation to the significance of intellectual processes of a certain quality in some obsessional neurosis. Freud said:

> Obsessional neurosis is shown in the patient's being occupied with thoughts in which he is in fact not interested, in his being aware of impulses in himself which appear very strange to him and in his being led to actions the performance of which give him no enjoyment, but which it is quite impossible for him to omit. The thoughts (obsessions) may be senseless in themselves, or merely a matter of indifference to the subject; often they are completely silly, and invariably they are the starting-point of a strenuous mental activity, which exhausts the patient and to which he only surrenders

himself most unwillingly. He is obliged against his will to brood and speculate as thought it were a question of his most important vital problems. . . . [1916x, p. 258]

Ambivalence in obsessional neuroses. Marked "ambivalent" feelings in relation to the same object is another important characteristic of obsessional neurosis, ". . . the chronic co-existence of love and hatred both directed towards the same person and both of the highest degree of intensity, cannot fail to astonish us" (1909d, p. 239). He continued:

And in fact such a protracted survival of two opposites is only possible under quite peculiar psychological conditions and with the co-operation of the state of affairs in the unconscious. The love has not succeeded in extinguishing the hatred but only in driving it down into the unconscious; and in the unconscious the hatred, safe from the danger of being destroyed by the operations of consciousness, is able to persist and even to grow. In such circumstances the conscious love attains as a rule, by way of reaction, an especially high degree of intensity, as to be strong enough for the perpetual task of keeping its opponent under repression. The necessary condition for the occurrence of such a strange state of affairs in a person's erotic life appears to be that at a very early age, somewhere in the prehistoric period of his infancy, the two opposites should have been split apart and one of them, usually the hatred, have been repressed [p. 239].

Freud further thought that a certain amount of ambivalence is present in everybody, and a larger amount than usual is in any case a charactistic of neurotic people in general.

As we have pointed out before (See section on "Regression and Obsessional Neurosis") he hesitated between considering it a product of defusion (due to the regression to anal-sadism in obsessional neurosis) or as representing a lack of sufficient instinctual fusion (1923d, p. 42).

Further, in *Inhibitions, Symptoms and Anxiety* (1926d) Freud explained how obsessionals manage to make the symptoms acquire in addition to the original meaning a directly opposite one: "This is a tribute to the power of ambivalence, which for some unknown reason plays such a large part in obsessional neuroses" (p. 113).

In "Notes Upon a Case of Obsessional Neurosis" (1909d) he had stated that the relationship between love and hate is perhaps the most important characteristic of obsessional neurosis (p. 239).

Omnipotence in obsessional neuroses. Freud has made it clear that in symptom formation and neurotic development what is important is the "psychic reality" of the patient and not "external reality"; as he put it, "the reality not of experience but of thought." He continued: "Neurotics live in a world apart, where . . . only 'neurotic currency' is legal tender; that is to say, they are only affected by what is thought with intensity and pictured with emotion, whereas agreement with external reality is a matter of no importance (1912x, p. 86).

This is particularly the case with obsessional neurosis, one of whose main characteristics is the belief in the omnipotence of thoughts. Such a belief plays a very important role in this illness and can explain the intensity of the guilt and extreme reactions of the superego. This degree of guilt and super-ego reaction "has a justification if what we take into account are unconscious thoughts and not intentional deeds" [i.e. the intense unconscious death wishes and aggressive phantasies of the obsessional]. Freud said: It is in obsessional neuroses that the survival of the omnipotence of thoughts is most clearly visible and that the consequences of this primitive mode of thinking come closest to consciousness" (1912x, p. 86).

A few years earlier, in "Notes Upon a Case of Obsessional Neurosis" (1909d), while discussing some aspects of the case, he referred to a somewhat puzzling trait of the patient. He said: "I refer to the *omnipotence* which he ascribed to his thoughts and feelings, and to his wishes, whether good or evil" (p. 233). He continued: "Indeed, all obsessional neurotics behave as though they shared this conviction" (p. 242).

Doubt and obsessional neuroses. A special characteristic or symptom of obsessional neurotics is their need for uncertainty and doubt. In "Notes Upon a Case of Obsessional Neurosis" (1909d), Freud made this observation:

Another mental need, which is also shared by obsessional neurotics . . . is the need for *uncertainty* in their life, or for doubt. . . . [A] predilection felt by obsessional neurotics for uncertainty and doubt leads them to turn their thoughts by perference to those subjects upon which all mankind are uncertain and upon which our knowledge and judgments must necessarily remain open to doubt. The chief subjects of this kind are paternity, length of life, life after death, and memory—in the last of which we are all in the habit of believing, without having the slightest guarantee of its trustworthiness. [p. 232]

Later on in the same paper he noted that "the *doubt* corresponds to the patient's internal perception of his own indecision, which, in consequence of the inhibition of his love by his hatred, takes possession of him in the face of every intended action. The doubt is in reality a doubt of his own love . . . (p. 242). And still later: "When the obsessional patient lays his finger on the weak spot in the security of our mental life—of the untrustworthiness of memory—the discovery enables him to extend his doubt over everything, even over actions which have already been performed and which have so far had no connection with the love-hatred complex, and over the entire past" (p. 243).

In the *Introductory Lectures on Psycho-Analysis* (1916x): "Alongside of obsessions with a positive and negative content, *doubt* makes itself felt in the intellectual field and little by little it begins to gnaw even at what is usually most certain. The whole position ends up in an ever-increasing degree of indecision, loss of energy and restriction of freedom" (pp. 259-260). The uncertainty and the doubt become attached as well to the performance of the compulsive actions themselves; there is always ". . . an apprehension that things might not have been done properly. Everything must be checked and repeated, doubts assailed, first one and then another, of the safety measures, and the result was that one or two hours were spent [checking and repeating the protective measures because of doubting] . . ." (p. 266).

Ego Development and Obsessional Neuroses

In his paper "The Disposition to Obsessional Neurosis," (1913i)—where he described for the first time the anal stage of pregenital sexual organization—he pointed to gaps in our knowledge of the developmental disposition to neurosis. He said that "the developmental disposition to a neurosis is only complete if the phase of the development of the ego at which fixation occurs is taken into account as well as that of the libido. But our hypothesis has only related to the latter, and, therefore, does not include all the knowledge that we should demand." He admitted that analysts knew little as yet about his aspect, and continued:

I cannot tell if it may seem too rash if, on the basis of such indications as we possess, I suggest the possibility that a chronological outstripping of libidinal development by ego development should be included in the disposition to obsessional neurosis. A precocity of this kind would necessitate the choice of an object under the influence of the ego-instincts, at a time at which the sexual instincts had not yet assumed their final shape, and a fixation at the stage of the pregenital sexual organization would thus be left. If we consider that obsessional neurotics have to develop a super-morality in order to protect their object-love from the hostility lurking behind it, we shall be inclined to regard some degree of this precocity of ego development as typical of human nature and to derive the capacity for the origin of morality from the fact that in the order of development hate is the precursor of love. [p. 325]

In *Inhibitions, Symptoms and Anxiety* (1926d), while attempting to explain the all-important regression to the anal-sadistic stage Freud thought that the latter was perhaps related to an early opposition of the ego to anality, that is, an opposition that starts while the anal-sadistic phase is at its height (pp. 113-114). (See section on "Repression.")

In the *Introductory Lectures on Psycho-Analysis,* (1916x), he stated that "the obsessional neurotic . . . is often extraordinarily self-willed and as a rule he has intellectual gifts above the average" (p. 260). Freud continues: "He has usually reached a satisfactorily high level of ethical development; he exhibits overconscientiousness, and is more than ordinarily correct in his behaviour" (p. 260).

In "Notes Upon a Case of Obsessional Neuroses" (1909d) he said: "The histories of obsessional patients almost invariably reveal an early development and premature repression of the instinct of looking and knowing . . ." (p. 245).

Superego and Obsessional Neuroses

The severity of the superego in obsessional neurosis is one of the main characteristics of this illness. Freud said:

We can either simply accept it as a fact that in obsessional neurosis a super-ego of this severe kind emerges, or we can take the regression of the libido as the fundamental characteristic of the affection and attempt to relate the severity of the super-ego to it. And indeed the super-ego, originating as it does from the id, cannot dissociate itself from the regression and defusion of instinct which have taken place there. We cannot be surprised if it becomes harsher, unkinder and more tormenting than where development has been normal. [1926d, pp. 115-116]

In *The Ego and the Id* (1923b) he stated that in obsessional neurosis

the defusion of love into aggressiveness has not been effected by the work of the ego, but is the result of a regression which has come about in the id. But this process has extended beyond the id to the super-ego, which now increased its severity towards the innocent ego. It would seem, however, that in this case, no less than in that of melancholia, the ego, having gained control over the libido by means of identification, is punished for doing so by the super-ego through the instrumentality of the aggressiveness which was mixed with the libido. [p. 55]

Further:

In certain forms of obsessional neurosis the sense of guilt is over-noisy but cannot justify itself to the ego. Consequently the patient's ego rebels against the imputation of guilt and seeks the physician's support in repudiating it. It would be folly to acquiesce in this, for to do so would have no effect. Analysis eventually shows that the super-ego is being influenced by processes that have remained unknown to the ego. It is possible to discover the repressed impulses which are really at the bottom of the sense of guilt. Thus in this case the super-ego knew more than the ego about the unconscious. [p. 51]

In *Inhibitions, Symptoms and Anxiety* (1926d) he came back to the same question:

The super-ego behaves as though repression had not occurred and as though it knew the real wording and full affective character of the aggressive impulse, and it treats the ego accordingly. The ego which, on the one hand, knows that it is innocent, is obliged, on the other hand, to be aware of a sense of guilt and to carry a responsibility which it cannot account for. This state of affairs is, however, not so puzzling as it would seem at first sight. The behaviour of the super-ego is perfectly intelligible, and the contradiction in the ego merely shows that it has shut out the id by means of repression while remaining fully accessible to the influence of the super-ego. If it is asked why the ego does not also attempt to withdraw from the tormenting criticism of the super-ego, the answer is that it *does* manage to do so in a great number of instances. There are obsessional neuroses in which no sense of guilt whatever is present. In them, as far as can be seen, the ego has avoided becoming aware of it by instituting a fresh set of symptoms, penances or restrictions of a self-punishing kind. [p. 117]

Freud pointed out why, in spite of the fact that the severity of the guilt and of the superego in obsessionals is similar to melancholia, there is no risk of suicide in this illness:

The reproaches of conscience in certain forms of obsessional neurosis are as distressing and tormenting [as in melancholia], but here the situation is less perspicuous. It is noteworthy that the obsessional neurotic, in contrast to the melancholic, never in fact takes the step of self-destruction; it is as though he were immune against the danger of suicide, and he is far better protected from it than the hysteric. We can see that what guarantees the safety of the ego is the fact that the object has been retained. In obsessional neurosis it has become possible, through regression to the pre-genital organization, for the love-impulses to transform themselves into impulses of aggression against the object. Here again the instinct of destruction has been set free and it seeks to destroy the object, or at least it appears to have that intention. These purposes have not been adopted by the ego and it struggles against them with reaction-formations and precautionary measures; they remain in the id. The super-ego, however, behaves as if the ego were responsible for them and shows at the same time by the seriousness with which it chastises these destructive intentions that they are no mere semblance evoked by regression but an actual substitution of hate for love. [1923b, pp. 53-54]

Similarly, the regression forces the emergence of some libidinal impulses as aggressive and destructive tendencies and:

In consequence of the erotic trends being disguised in this way and owing to the powerful reaction-formation in the ego, the struggle against sexuality will hence-forward be carried on under the banner of ethical principles. The ego will recoil with astonishment from promptings to cruelty and violence which enter consciousness from the id, and it has no notion that in them it is combating erotic wishes, including some to which it would not otherwise have taken exception. The overstrict super-ego insists all the more strongly on the suppression of sexuality, since this has assumed such repellent forms. Thus in obsessional neurosis the conflict is aggravated in two directions: the defensive forces become more intolerant and the forces that are to be fended off become intolerable. Both affects are due to a single factor, namely, regression of the libido. [1962d, pp. 116-117]

Freud pointed out the role that hysterical reality has to play in obsessional neuroses:

It is not accurate to say that obsessional neurotics, weighed down under the burden of an excessive morality, are defending themselves for impulses which were merely *felt*. Historical reality has a share in the matter as well. In their childhood they had these evil impulses pure and simple, and turned them into acts so far as the impotence of childhood allowed. . . .[1912x, pp. 160-161]

As a matter of interest we refer to a passage in Jones's biography of Freud (1955) where he says that the latter in a letter to Ferenczi mentioned casually, "that an intuition had disclosed the censorship in the obsessional neurosis as functioning between the preconscious and consciousness rather than between the unconscious and the preconscious" (p. 206).

Defenses and Obsessional Neuroses

Freud frequently compared the difference in defense activities to be observed between hysteria and obsessional neurosis. The former makes use largely of the mechanism of repression, while the latter tends to use a number of other defense mechanisms. With the use of repression in hysteria significant events or mental contents are overtaken by amnesia and this is not often the case in obsessional neurosis: experience is not forgotten but the affect is taken away from the idea, so that the final effect is similar in some ways to that of repression with amnesia.

As will be seen below Freud referred to a number of specific defense mechanisms as typical of the obsessional neurosis. Isolation of content and affect, undoing, reaction-formation and displacement play an essential role in this illness and in the mechanism of symptom formation.

Repression itself does have a place in obsessional neurosis. That and its interaction and simultaneous combination with other defense mechanisms in obsessionals are aspects of Freud's formulations that have been somewhat neglected.

It should be noted that for many years, and certainly in Freud's early papers dealing with obsessional neurosis, the word repression is frequently used not in the sense of the specific defense mechanisms we are familiar with but as synonymous with defense. This can lead to a certain amount of confusion since he may use the term to refer to defense mechanisms such as reaction-formation, isolation, etc.

Finally it should be noted that in regard to obsessional neurosis the ceremonial itself starts as an action for defense.

When the ceremonial is first being constructed, the patient is still conscious that he must do this or that lest some ill should befall, and as a rule the nature of the ill that is to be expected is still known to his consciousness. But what is already hidden from him is the connection—which is always demonstrable—between the occasion on which this expectant anxiety arises and the danger which it conjures up. Thus a ceremonial starts as an *action for defence or insurance,* a *protective measure.* [1907b, p. 123]

Repression. As we have seen above, the term *repression* has been used with more than one meaning. But from the quotations that follow, a number of points will be quite clear in any case:

1. We find Freud wondering about the possibility that other and typical defense mechanisms of obsessionals result from a failure of repression in its functioning.
2. He seems to use "repression" to cover both repression proper and repression as synonymous with defense, in one and the same quotations.
3. Repression proper is used in obsessional neurosis especially in trying to deal with the hostile regressive anal-sadistic impulses, at least during the first state of the defense activity.

In *Inhibitions, Symptoms and Anxiety* (1926d) Freud suggested that "the fact that such auxiliary and substitutive techniques emerge [undoing and isolating] may argue that true repression has met with difficulties in its functioning" (p. 119).

In his paper "Repression" (1915d) he discusses the vicissitudes in anxiety hysteria, conversion hysteria, and obsessional neurosis of both the ideational content and the affect attached to the latter in the process of repression.

In *anxiety hysteria* he uses as an example an animal phobia resulting from the repression of a libidinal attitude toward the father coupled with fear of him the instinctual impulse after repression "vanishes out of consciousness: the father does not appear in it as an object of libido"

(1915d, p. 155). He goes on to say that as a substitute for the father an animal will be used (by means of a chain of *displacements*). The affect ("quantitative portion") has not vanished in anxiety hysteria but is transformed in "anxiety." Repression in this case has been unsuccessful; all it has done is replace the idea, while at the same time failing to avoid unpleasure.

In *conversion hysteria* the important point is that through repression "it is possible to bring about a total disappearance of the quota of affect" (p. 155). This leads to an attitude toward the symptom described by Charcot as "la belle indifférence des hystériques" (p. 156). There are of course cases where the repression is not so successful and some releases of anxiety may occur and even lead to phobic reaction. The "ideational content" of the instinctual representative is in conversion hysteria replaced by a substitute which is in this case at the same time a symptom. Repression in conversion hysteria is unsuccessful insofar as it only deals with the ideational content by forming displaced substitutes, but "as regards dealing with the quota of affect . . . which is the true task of repression, it generally signifies a total success" (p. 156).

In *obsessional neurosis* after making clear that what is subjected to repression is the regressive "hostile impulsion against someone who is loved" (p. 156), Freud continues by saying that in obsessionals "at first the repression is completely successful; the ideational content is rejected and the affect made to disappear. As a substitutive formation there arises an alteration in the ego in the shape of an increased conscientiousness, and this can hardly be called a symptom. Here substitute and symptom do not coincide [as they do in conversion hysteria]" (p. 157). The "substitute formation" is arrived at in obsessionals thanks to the mechanism of "reaction formation" by intensifying an opposite (while in anxiety and conversion hysteria the "substitute formation" is arrived at by means of "displacement" and is usually of the nature of a symptom). Freud thinks that this whole process is rendered possible in obsessionals because of the ambivalence in the relationship. He continues:

But the repression, which was at first successful, does not hold firm; in the further course of things its failure becomes increasingly marked. The ambivalence which has enabled repression through reaction-formation to take place is also the point at which the repressed succeeds in returning. The vanished affect comes back in its transformed shape as social anxiety, moral anxiety and unlimited self-reproaches; the rejected idea is replaced by a *substitute by displacement,* often a displacement onto something very small or indifferent. A tendency to a complete reestablishment of the repressed idea is as a rule unmistakably present. The failure in the repression of the quantitative, affective factor brings into play the same mechanism of flight, by means of avoidance and prohibitions, as we have seen at work in the formation of hysterial phobias. The rejection of the *idea* from the conscious is, however, obstinately maintained, because it entails abstention from action, a motor fettering of the impulse. Thus in obsessional neurosis the work of repression is prolonged in a sterile and interminable struggle. [p. 157]

Earlier, in 1909, he said:

In hysteria it is the rule that the precipitating causes of the illness are overtaken by amnesia no less than the infantile experiences by whose help the precipitating causes are able to transform their affective energy into symptoms. . . . The case is different obsessional neuroses. The infantile peconditions of the neurosis may be overtaken by amnesia, though this is often an incomplete one; but the immediate occasions of the illness are, on the contrary, retained in the memory. Repression [this is a good example of the term *repression* being used as synonymous with defense] makes use of another, and in reality a simple, mechanism. The trauma, instead of being forgotten, is deprived of its affective cathexis [isolation of affect]; so that what remains in consciousness is nothing but is ideational content, which is perfectly colourless and is judged to be unimportant. . . . In order to differentiate between the two kinds of repression we have on the surface nothing to rely upon but the patient's assurance that he has a feeling in the one case of having always known the thing and in the other of having long ago forgotten it. [1909d, pp. 195-196]

Reaction-formation. "In obsessional neurosis, as we know, the phenomena of reaction-formation predominate . . ."(1923b, p. 52).

"The reaction-formations in the ego of the obsessional neurotic, which we recognize as exaggerations of normal character-formation, would be regarded, I think, as yet another mechanism of defence and placed alongside of regresssion and repression. They seem to be absent or much weaker in hysteria" (1926d, p. 115).

In *Moses and Monotheism,* (1939a), Freud further characterized the obsessional neurotic reaction-formations. He does so while explaining the ethical heights reached—in doctrine and precept at least—by Judaism. He said: "These ethical ideas cannot, however, disavow their origin from the sense of guilt felt on account of suppressed hostility to God. They possess the characteristic—incompleted and incapable of completion—of obsessional neurotic reaction formations . . ." (1939a, pp. 134-135).

Undoing. Freud refers to undoing (and isolation) as auxiliary and substitutive defensive techniques of the ego when repression has not worked properly.

[Undoing] has a wide range of application and goes back very far. It is, as it were, negative magic, and endeavours, by means of motor symbolism, to "blow away" not merely the *consequences* of some event (or experience or impression) but the event itself. I choose the term "blow away" advisedly, so as to remind the reader of the part played by this technique not only in neuroses by in magical acts, popular customs and religious ceremonies as well. In obsessional neurosis the technique of undoing what has been done is first met with in the "diphasic" symptoms, in which one action is cancelled out by a second, so that it is as though neither action had taken place, whereas in reality both have. This aim of undoing is the second underlying motive of obsessional ceremonials, the first being to take precautions in order to prevent the occurrence or recurrence of some particular event. The difference between the two is easily seen: The precautionary measures are rational, while trying to get rid of something by "making it not to have happened" is irrational and in the nature of magic. It is of course to be suspected that the latter is the earlier motive of the two and proceeds from the animistic attitude towards the environment. This endeavor to undo shades off into normal behaviour in the case in which a person decides to regard an event as not having happened. But whereas he will take no direct steps against the event, and will simply pay no further attention to it or its consequences, the neurotic person will try to make the past itself non-existent. He will try to repress it by motor means. The same purpose may perhaps account for the obsession for *repeating* which is so frequently met with in this neurosis and the carrying out of which serves a number of contradictory intentions at once. When anything has not happened in the desired way it is undone by being repeated in a different way; and thereupon all the motives that exist for lingering over such repetitions come into play as well. As the neurosis proceeds, we often find that the endeavour to undo a traumatic experience is a motive of first-rate importance in the formation of symptoms. We thus unexpectedly discover a new, motor technique of defence, or (as we may say in this case with less inaccuracy) of repression. [1926d, pp. 119-120]

This defense had in fact already been described in "Notes Upon a Case of Obsessional Neurosis" (1909d) though the term "undoing" was not used then: "Compulsive acts like this, in two successive stages, of which the second neutralises the first, are a typical occurrence in obsessional neuroses" (p. 192).

Isolation of Affect. This particular defense mechanism was described as early as 1894 in "The Neuro-Psychoses of Defence" as characteristic for the development of "obsessional ideas."

If someone with a disposition [to neurosis] lacks the aptitude for conversion, but if, nevertheless, in order to fend off an incompatible idea, he sets about separating it from its affect, then *that affect is obliged to remain in the psychical sphere*. The idea, now weakened, is still left in consciousness, separated from all association. *But its affect, which has become free, attaches itself to other ideas which are not in themselves incompatible; and, thanks to the "false connection," those ideas turn into obsessional ideas.* [1894a, pp. 51-52]

In *Inhibitions, Symptoms and Anxiety* (1926d) Freud stated:

The second of these techniques which we are setting out to describe for the first time, that of isolation, is peculiar to obsessional neurosis. It, too, takes place in the motor sphere. When something unpleasant has happened to the subject or when he himself has done something which has a significance for his neurosis, he interpolates an interval during which nothing further must happen—during which he must perceive nothing and do nothing. This behaviour, which seems strange at first sight, is soon seen to have a relation to repression. We know that in hysteria it is possible to cause a traumatic experience to be overtaken by amnesia. In obsessional neurosis this can often not be achieved: the experience is not forgotten, but, instead, it is deprived of its affect, and its associative connections are suppressed or interrupted so that it remains as though isolated and is not reproduced in the ordinary processes of thought. The effect of this isolation is the same as the effect of repression with amnesia. This technique, then, is reproduced in the isolations of obsessional neurosis; and it is at the same time given motor reinforcement for magical purposes. The elements that are held apart in this way are precisely those which belong together associatively. The motor isolation is meant to ensure an interruption of the connection in thought. [pp. 120-121]

Isolation of Content. Of one of the most favored mechanisms used by obsessionals, Freud (1914g) said: "In the many different forms of obsessional neurosis in particular, forgetting is mostly restricted to dissolving thought-connections, failing to draw the right conclusions and isolating memories" (p. 149).

Displacement. This essential defense mechanism of obsessional neurosis explains the fact that many of the obsessional ideas and ceremonials seem concerned with "small actions of daily life and are expressed in foolish regulations and restrictions in connection with them." Freud continued:

We cannot understand this remarkable feature of the clinical picture until we have realised that the mechanism of psychical *displace-*

ment, which was first discovered by me in the construction of dreams, dominates the mental processes of obsessional neurosis. . . . Their symbolism [that of obsessive actions] and the detail of their execution are brought about by a displacement from the actual important thing onto a small one which takes its place—for instance, from a husband onto a chair. It is this tendency to displacement which progressively changes the clinical picture and eventually succeeds in turning what is apparently the most trivial matter into something of the utmost importance and urgency. [1907b, pp. 125-126]

In the *Introductory Lectures on Psycho-Analysis* (1916x), while talking about the peculiar form of energy that seems to sustain the symptoms in obsessional neurosis, Freud stated:

There is only one thing he [the obsessional neurotic] can do: he can make displacements and exchanges, he can replace one foolish idea by another somewhat milder, he can proceed from one precaution or prohibition to another, instead of one ceremonial he can perform another. He can displace the obsession but not remove it. The ability to displace any symptom into something far removed from its original conformation is a main characteristic of his illness. [p. 259]

The Mechanism of Symptom Formation

The mechanism of symptom formation in the obsessional neurosis is a very complex proposition in which multiple factors interact and combine. In this chapter only a limited number of these will be considered, since in many of the other sections the role of one or another factor in the formation of symptoms will become apparent— for example, that of these defense mechanisms typical of obsessionals: anal sadistic regression, ambivalence, defusion, and severity of the superego.

As early as 1896, in Chapter II ("The Nature and Mechanisms of Obsessional Neurosis") of his paper "Further Remarks On the Neuro-Psychoses of Defence," Freud described the typical course taken by the illness in its four periods: the first period, the period of childhood immorality, with the early passive seduction and the later active one;

the second period, starting with "sexual maturation," at which point the seductive experiences are repressed and replaced by a "primary symptom of defense" such as conscientiousness, shame, or self-distrust; the third period, one of successful defense and apparent health; and the fourth period, that of the return of the repressed memories because of the breakdown of defenses. A compromise is then reached between the repressed ideas and the repressing ones, which compromise become the conscious obsessional ideas and affects. (For the full quotation of the above passage see the section "Etiological Considerations"). Freud then went on to explain the different clinical forms, obsessional ideas, obsessional affects, and obsessional actions with all their variations and the mechanisms and ideational contents behind them (1896b, pp. 169-174; see also the section "Types of Obsessional Neurosis"). He refers, for example, to how the contents of the obsessional ideas have been distorted:

> First something contemporary is put in the place of something past, and secondly, something sexual is replaced by something analogous to it that is not sexual. These two alterations are the effect of the inclination to repress, still in force, which we will ascribe to the "ego."
>
> The influence of the re-activated pathogenic memory is shown by the fact that the content of the obsessional idea is still in part identical with what has been repressed or follows from it by a logical train of thought. If, with the help of the psycho-analytic method, we reconstruct the origin of an individual obsessional idea, we find that from a single current impression two different trains of thought have been set going. The one which has passed by way of the repressed memory proves to be as correctly logical in its structure as the other, although it is incapable of being conscious and insusceptible to correction. If the products of the two psychical operations do not tally, what takes place is not some sort of logical adjustment of the contradictions between them; instead, alongside of the *normal* intellectual outcome, there comes into consciousness, as a compromise between the resistance and the *pathological* intellectual product, an obsessional idea which appears absurd. If the two trains of thought lead to the *same* conclusion, they reinforce each other, so

that an intellectual product that has been arrived at normally now behaves, psychologically, like an obsessional idea. *Whenever a neurotic obsession emerges in the psychical sphere, it comes from repression.* Obsessional ideas have, as it were, a compulsive psychical currency, not on account of their intrinsic value, but on account of the source from which they derive which has added a contribution to their value. [pp. 170-171]

In his paper "Obsessive Actions and Religious Practices" (1907b) he establishes the important link between many of the obsessional symptoms and the "unconscious sense of guilt." After describing how the analysis of obsessive actions has helped to explain their causes and the chain of motives which bring them into effect, he added:

We may say that the sufferer from compulsions and prohibitions behaves as if he were dominated by a sense of guilt, of which, however, he knows nothing, so that we must call it an unconscious sense of guilt, in spite of the apparent contradiction in terms. This sense of guilt has its source in certain early mental events, but it is constantly being revived by renewed temptations which arise whenever there is a contemporary provocation. Moreover, it occasions a lurking sense of expectant anxiety, an expectation of misfortune which is linked, through the idea of punishment, with the internal perception of the temptation. When the ceremonial is first being constructed, the patient is still conscious that he must do this or that lest some ill should befall, and as a rule the nature of the ill that is to be expected is still known to his consciousness. But what is already hidden from him is the connection—which is always demonstrable—between the occasion on which this expectant anxiety arises and the danger which it conjures up. Thus a ceremonial starts as an *action for defence* or *insurance,* a *protective measure.* The sense of guilt of obsessional neurotics finds its counterpart in the protestations of pious people that they know that at heart they are miserable sinners; and the pious observances (such as prayers, invocations, etc.) with which such people preface every daily act, and in especial every unusual undertaking, seem to have the value of defensive or protective measures. [1907b, pp. 123-124]

In "Notes Upon a Case of Obsessional Neurosis" (1909d), he referred to certain compulsive acts which are theoretically of special interest, showing us a new method of constructing symptoms. He refers to those compulsive actions, in two stages of which the second neutralizes the first. He points out how here each one of two opposing tendencies finds satisfaction individually, and one after the other, while usually in hysteria the two tendencies find expression simultaneously in the form of a compromise symptom (p. 192; for the full quotation see the section "Obsessional Neurosis and Hysteria").

In the same paper Freud notes the role of distortion in the obsessional structures and its similarities with the processes that take place in the dream:

> One becomes convinced that if a number of obsessions succeed one another they are often—even though their wording is not identical—ultimately one and the same. The obsession may have been successfully shaken off on its first appearance, but it comes back a second time in a distorted form and without being recognized, and may then perhaps be able to hold its own in the defensive struggle more effectively, precisely because of its distortion.... What is officially described as an "obsessional idea" exhibits, therefore, in its distortion from its original wording, traces of the primary defensive struggle, Its distortion enables it to persist, since conscious thought is thus compelled to misapprehend it, just as though it were a dream; for dreams also are a product of compromise and distortion, and are also misapprehended by waking thought. [pp. 223-224]

[Distortion] is not the only means employed. In addition each separate obsessional idea is almost invariably removed from the situation in which it originated and in which, in spite of its distortion, it would be most easily comprehensible. With this end in view, in the first place *an interval of time is inserted* between the pathogenic situation and the obsession that arises from it, so as to lead astray any conscious investigation of its causal connections, and in the second place the content of the obsession is taken out of its particular setting by being *generalised*. . . . Finally, if we care to distinguish verbal distortion from distortion of content, there is yet another means by which the obsession is protected against conscious attempts at solution. And that is the choice of an indefinite or ambiguous wording. After being misunderstood, the wording may find its way into the patient's "deliria,"and whatever further processes of development or substitution his obsession undergoes will then be based upon the misunderstanding and not upon the proper sense of the text. Observation will show, however, that the deliria constantly tend to form new connections with that part of the matter and wording of the obsession which is not present in consciousness. [pp. 246-247]

In the same paper, Freud says that the "technique of distortion by ellipsis seems to be typical of obsessional neuroses . . ." (p. 227).

Symptoms are always the result of conflict, defense activity and compromises of different sorts between the forces involved. It is thus particularly important to point to the following fact. Freud says:

I will only add that in obsessional neuroses the unconscious mental processes occasionally break through into consciousness in their pure and undistorted form, that such incursions may take place at every possible stage of the unconscious process of thought, and that at the moment of the incursion the obsessional ideas can, for the most part, be recognized as formation of very long standing. This accounts for the striking circumstance that, when the analyst tries with the patient's help to discover the date of the first occurrence of an obsessional idea, the patient is obliged to place it further and further back as the analysis proceeds, and is constantly finding fresh "first" occasions for the appearance of the obsession. [pp. 228-229]

In his book *Totem and Taboo* (1912x) Freud explains how it happens that the prohibitions of obsessionals tend to spread:

The prohibition [in obsessionals] owes its strength and its obsessive character precisely to its unconscious opponent, the concealed and undiminished desire—that is to say, to an internal necessity inaccessible to conscious inspection. The ease with which the prohibition can be transferred and extended reflects a process which falls in with the unconscious desire and is greatly facilitated by the psychologcal conditions that prevail in the unconscious. The instinctual desire is constantly shifting in order to escape from the *impasse* and endeavours to find substitutes—substitute objects and substitute acts—in place of the prohibited ones. In consequence of this, the prohibition itself shifts about as well, and extends to any new aims which the forbidden impulse may adopt. Any fresh advance made by the repressed libido is answered by a fresh sharpening of the prohibition. The mutual inhibition of the two conflicting forces produces a need for discharge, for reducing the prevailing tension; and to this may be attributed the reason for the performance of obsessive acts. In the case of a neurotic these are clearly compromise actions: from one point of view thay are evidences of remorse, efforts at expiration and so on, while on the other hand they are at the same time substitutive acts to compensate the instinct for what has been prohibited. It is a law of neurotic illness that these obsessive acts fall more and more under the sway of the instinct and approach nearer and nearer to the activity which was originally prohibited. [p. 30]

In *Inhibitions, Symptoms and Anxiety* (1962d) he discusses further the question of symptom formation:

Let us turn to the obsessional neuroses in the hope of learning more about the formation of symptoms. The symptoms belonging to this neurosis fall, in general, into two groups, each having an opposite trend. They are either prohibitions, precautions and expiations— that is, negative in character—or they are, on the contrary, substitutive satisfactions which often appear in symbolic disguise. The negative, defensive group of symptoms is the older of the two; but as illness is prolonged, the satisfactions, which scoff at all defensive measures, gain the upper hand. The symptom-formation scores a triumph if it succeeds in combining the prohibition with satisfaction so that what was originally a defensive command or prohibition acquires the significance of a satisfaction as well and in order to achieve this end it will often make use of the most ingenious associative paths. Such an achievement demonstrates the tendency of the ego to synthesize. . . . In extreme cases the patient manages to make most of his symptoms acquire, in addition to their original meaning, a directly contrary one. This is a tribute to the power of ambivalence, which for some unknown reason, plays such a large part in obsessional neuroses. In the crudest instance the symptom is diphasic: an action which carries out a certain injunction is immediately succeeded by another action which stops or undoes the first one even if it does not go quite so far as to carry out its opposite. [pp. 112-113]

He then arrives at the following conclusions:

Two impressions at once emerge from this brief survey of obsessional symptoms. The first is that a ceaseless struggle is being waged against the repressed, in which the repressing forces steadily lose ground; the second is that the ego and the super-ego have a specially large share in the formation of the symptoms. [p. 113]

In the same book Freud points out that

the general tendency of symptom-formation in obsessional neurosis ... is to give ever greater room to substitutive satisfaction at the expense of frustration. Symptoms which once stood for a restriction of the ego come later on to represent satisfaction as well, thanks to the ego's inclination to synthesis, and it is quite clear that this second meaning gradually becomes the more important of the two. The result of this process, which approximates more and more to a complete failure of the original purpose of defence, is an extremely restricted ego which is reduced to seeking satisfaction in the symptoms. The displacement of the distribution of forces in favour of satisfaction may have the dreaded final outcome of paralysing the will of the ego, which in every decision it has to make is almost as strongly impelled from the one side as from the other. The over-acute conflict between id and super-ego which has dominated the illness from the very beginning may assume such extensive proportions that the ego, unable to carry out its office of mediator, can undertake nothing which is not drawn into the sphere of that conflict. [p. 118]

He continues: "In the course of these struggles we come across two activities of the ego which form symptoms and which deserve special attention because they are obviously surrogates of repression and, therefore, well calculated to illustrate its purpose and technique." He is referring here to the defense mechanisms of undoing what has been done and isolating it (p. 119). (For the role played by these and other defenses see the sections "Defences and Obsessional Neuroses;" "Displacement;" "Undoing;" "Isolation of Affect;" "Reaction-Formations;" "Repression and Regression in Obsessional Neuroses".)

Finally, Freud not infrequently made comparisons between the mechanisms in obsessional neurosis and in religious practices. In "Obsessive Actions and Religious Practices" (1907b), he concluded that

In view of the similarities and analogies one might venture to regard obsessional neurosis as a pathological counterpart of the formation of a religion, and to describe that neurosis as an individual religiosity, and religion as a universal obsessional neurosis. The most essential similarity [between obsessional neurosis and religion] would reside in the underlying renunciation of the activation of instincts that are constitutionally present; and the chief difference would lie in the nature of those instincts, which in the neurosis are exclusively sexual in their origin, while in religion they spring from egoistic sources. [p. 126; see also Freud, 1912x]

In the same paper he said:

A further characteristic of obsessional neurosis, as of all similar affections, is that its manifestations (its symptoms, including the obsessive actions) fulfill the condition of being a compromise between the warring forces of the mind. They thus always reproduce something of the pleasure which they are designed to prevent; they serve the repressed instinct no less than the agencies which are repressing it. As the illness progresses, indeed, actions which were originally mostly concerned with maintaining the defence come to approximate more and more to the prescribed actions through which the instinct was able to find expression in childhood. . . . The formation of a religion, too, seems to be based on the suppression, the renunciation of certain instinctual impulses. . . . A sense of guilt following upon continual temptation and an expectant anxiety in the form of fear of divine punishment have, after all, been familiar to us in the field of religion longer than in that of the neurosis. Perhaps because of the admixture of sexual components, perhaps because of some general characteristics of the instincts, the suppression of instinct proves to be an inadequate and interminable process in religious life also. [p. 125]

It seems appropriate to end this section with a statement Freud made while dealing with the question of symptom formation in obsessionals, in *Inhibitions, Symptoms and Anxiety* (1926d):

Obsessional neurosis presents such a vast multiplicity of phenomena that no efforts have yet succeeded in making a coherent synthesis of all its variations. All we can do is to pick out certain typical correlations; but there is always the risk that we may have overlooked other uniformities of a no less important kind. [p. 118]

Obsessional Neuroses and Hysteria

Freud in his writings frequently compared these two clinical entities. In *Inhibitions, Symptoms and Anxiety* (1926d) he explained that "the ego is much more the scene of action of symptom-formation in obsessional neurosis than it is in hysteria . . ." (p. 119). He pointed out the many important differences of defense activities to be observed in these two clinical entities. Very briefly, the main defense mechanism in hysteria consists of repression, and it is for this reason that many significant events are overtaken by amnesia. In obsessionals this effect, because of the use of different defenses, is not always achieved, and the experiences are not necessarily forgotten or overcome by amnesia. As he points out in the *Introductory Lectures* (1916x), all that happens is that "a connection had been broken which ought to have led to the reproduction or re-emergence of the memory. A disturbance of memory of this kind is enough for obsessional neurosis, but the case is different with hysteria. As a rule the latter neurosis is marked by amnesias on a really large scale" (p. 283). (For further differences and similarities as to the work of repression in hysteria and obsessions see the section "Repression".)

Freud refers in the *Lectures* to certain specific and typical mechanisms of defense in obsessional neuroses and "variations of repression" or "surrogates of repression."He has in mind *"undoing what has been done and isolating"* (p. 119). The important role of reaction-formation and displacement in this illness was described in the section "Ego Defences" under the corresponding defense.

In his paper "The Unconscious" (1915e), Freud "ventures the supposition that it is because of the predominance of the anticathexis and the absence of discharge that the work of repression [here apparently used as synonymous with defense] seems far less successful in anxiety hysteria and in obsessional neurosis than in conversion hysteria" (p. 185).

One essential difference between obsessionals and hysterics consists in the regression that takes place in obsessionals to the anal-sadistic stage of development. "In obsessional neurosis . . . it is the regression of the libido to the preliminary stage of the sadistic-anal organisation that is the most striking fact and the one which is decisive for what is manifested in symptoms" (1916x, p. 343). (See above, "Regression Obsessional Neurosis".) In the hysteric patient there is no regression to a prephallic stage of drive organization. As he pointed out: ". . . there remains for hysteria an intimate relation to the final phase of libidinal development, which is characterised by the primacy of the genitals and the introduction of the reproductive function. In hysterical neurosis this acquisition is subjected to repression, which does not involve regression to the pregenital stage" (1913i, p. 325). And: "Now it is true that in hysteria there is a regression of the libido to the primary incestuous sexual objects and that this occurs quite regularly; but there is as good as no regression to an earlier stage of the sexual organisation. To offset this, the chief part in the mechanism of hysteria is played by repression" (1916x, p. 343).

He remarked on certain differences as to the symptoms produced as compromise formations in hysteria and obsessional neurosis:

Consequently symptoms are in the nature of compromises between the repressed sexual instincts and the repressing ego instincts; they represent a wish-fulfillment for both partners to the conflict simultaneously, but one which is incomplete for each of them. This is quite strictly true of the symptoms of hysteria, while in the symptoms of obsessional neurosis there is often a stronger emphasis upon the side of the repressing function owing to the erection of reaction-formations, which are assurances against sexual satisfactions. [1923a, p. 247]

And in "Notes Upon a Case of Obsessional Neurosis" (1909d), while referring to a type of compulsive act consisting of two successive states (typical of obsessionals) of which the second neutralizes the first he says:

Compulsive acts of this sort are theoretically of special interest, for *they show us a new type of method of constructing symptoms.* What regularly occurs in hysteria is that a compromise is arrived at which enables both the opposing tendencies to find expression simultaneously—which kills two birds with one stone; whereas here each of the two opposing tendencies finds satisfaction singly, first one and then the other, though naturally an attempt is made to establish some sort of logical connection (often in defiance of all logic) between the antagonists. [p. 192]

Similarly, in the *Introductory Lectures* (1916x), he remarks on the differences in symptom formation between hysterics and obsessionals. He says:

Even in obsessional neurosis there is much—apart from fundamentals, which remain unaltered—that will be found different. The anticathexes opposing the demands of the instincts (which we have already spoken of in the case of hysteria as well) become prominent in obsessional neurosis and dominate the clincial picture in the form of what are known as reaction-formations. [p. 375]

In *Inhibitions, Symptoms and Anxiety* (1926d) he stated that the reaction-formations in the ego of the obsessional are exaggerations of normal character formation and are to be considered as another defense mechanism of the illness, but they seem to be absent or to be much weaker in hysteria (p. 115). He indicated as well the affinity of hysteria and femininity, and obsessional neurosis and masculinity:

> Since there is no doubt that hysteria has a strong affinity with femininity, just as obsessional neurosis has with masculinity, it appears probably that as a determinant of anxiety, loss of love plays much the same part in hysteria as the threat of castration does in phobias and fear of the super-ego in obsessional neuroses. [p. 143]

In other chapters we have come across a few more explicit comparisons between hysterics and obsessionals that need not be repeated here. Many more could be inferred by we prefer to leave the inferences to the reader.

Chapter 2

Contributions by Other Analysts

It may come as a surprise that relatively few contributions in relation to obsessional neuroses are to be found in the psychoanalytic literature. In fact the bibliography on the subject, considering its importance, is rather limited. A few analysts have contributed fragments of analysis of obsessional neurosis or of specific aspects of these analyses, notably Ruth Max Brunswick, who contributed the analysis of the "Wolf Man" (1950). Similarly, Berta Bornstein (1953), Sandor Lorand (1947), Augusta Bonnard (1950), Ernest Jones (1912, and G. Pearson (1940) have published material from the analysis of cases of obsessional neuroses.

No attempt is made here to summarize the various authors' views as put forward in their publications. I have somewhat arbitrarily selected small vignettes from their papers that seem to me relevant in a review of the subject. I decided to do so because it was difficult to find much that was truly original. Much of the literature consists of repetitions, elaborations, or confirmations of Freud's (and a few others') points of view. Thus, not infrequently, I tended to single out ideas that seemed to me either different, fresh, or simply interesting. At other times I selected what seemed the central theme of the paper. Those interested in a review of the subject wider than the psychoanalytic can refer themselves to A. T. Carr's "Compulsive Neurosis: A Review of the Literature" (1974.) This paper contains fifty-three bibliographic references to obsessional neuroses from the behavioristic and other points of view I have not covered. The paper contains too some critical evaluations of the various models proposed for understanding obsessional neurosis. These include Freud's views on obsessional neurosis, which Carr discards rather lightly. It is clear in the paper that his understanding of Freud's formulations is rather limited. Also useful is D.I. Templer's "The Obsessive-Compulsive Neurosis: Review of Research Findings" (1972), which contains forty references to research findings in American and British literature.

Nunberg in his *Principles of Psychoanalysis* (1955) gives a fairly full survey of the psychoanalytic theory of the neuroses. While there is no chapter specifically devoted to obsessional neuroses, he has nevertheless incorporated in the different sections nearly all the essential contributions made by Freud to the theoretical and clincial understanding of the illness.

We have selected some of Numberg's formulations, in spite of their close coincidence with Freud's, because in the process of summarizing Freud's concepts Nunberg has made more clear their depth of meaning. There are also in his book many valuable comparisons between aspects of obsessionals, hysterics, phobics, melancholics, and schizophrenics.

Nunberg remarks on the fact that obsessional neurosis is hardly ever pure: "It frequently begins with hysteria, and also during its further course hysterical symptoms appear. *Hysteria often begins in childhood and is succeeded later, usually in puberty, by obsessional neurosis"* (author's emphasis) (p. 276).

He similarly states: "It is known, however, that there is no obsessional neurosis without a hysterical admixture; the hysterical symptoms of the compulsion neurosis manifest themselves, in my experience, primarily in the digestive tract" (p. 163).

He points to the fact that the obsessional neurosis uses autoplastic measures:

The obsessional neurotic, too, employs autoplastic measures in the solution of the neurotic conflict. The impulses of the id striving toward objects of the external world turn against the subject's own person, and instead of using the release psychic energy to change the external world, the obsessional neurotic changes his own character.

Just as the phobic believes that he can flee from the demands of the id with the help of the motor apparatus, so the obsessional neurotic believes that he can attain the same end by means of his precautionary measures, his magic formulas, and his ceremonial. [p. 248]

Nunberg thinks the obsessional suffers more from his illness than the hysteric does. He thinks this is due not only to the damming up of the libido, but to other factors as well:

The obsessional neurotic does not suffer only from frustration; there is evident in his symptomatology also a trait of self-torment. This contains the aggressive and destructive impulses which in the id are aimed at the object. The sadism directed against the object is turned against the subject, diverted onto the ego. The auto-sadism of the obsessional neurotic takes the form of self-reproaches, sacrifices, acts of expiation and castigation, and hence serves to gratify the need for punishment. Usually the obsessional neurotic permits a gratification of libidinal strivings only if he can, by the same token, punish himself. He has to pay for the pleasure with self-torment.

The gratification of the need for punishment is not characteristic of the obsessional neurosis exclusively. The need for punishment takes its toll in every neurosis. [p. 279]

Nunberg considers the effects of the regression on the potency of the obsessional neurotic:

The compulsive neurotic either renounces his genital function completely, or else his genital strivings are interspersed with strivings of the pre-genital stage, and he has coitus with the aid of anal and sadistic practices and fantasies.

In compulsion neurosis, therefore, the genital organization is regressively traversed, but it is not destroyed as in schizophrenia; the genital strivings which represent the unimpaired part of the phallic organization merely make use of the anal-sadistic urges and ideas, and do not return to this stage of development. Hence the compulsive neurotic is neither impotent nor manifestly perverse. [p. 105]

He discusses the question of the relationship to the object:

One might raise the question as to why the return of libido to a developmental phase in which the destructive instincts are still so powerful does not lead to the giving up of the objects altogether, that is, to a psychosis. Experience shows that the compulsive neurotic very early in life develops a strong attachment to a particular person in his immediate environment. This tie remains firm and continues to exist at the time of a fixation which occurs somewhat later in life. Only the regression that sets in with the outbreak of illness is capable of threatening even this tie. . . . In the compulsive neurotic, a libidinal attachment to an object is formed at a time when the rest of the sexual development is not yet corresponsdingly consolidated. In other words, the choice of an object occurs in advance of the sexual development and is impaired only when the regression occurs. The early libidinal attachment as well as the unrelinquished part of the phallic organization might be considered the decisive factors which cause the compulsive neurotic's resistance to a complete detachment of libido from the objects. It is true that after the regression, his attitude toward these objects is ambivalent, but still he fights continually for the possession of the object, which continues to exist for him, in contrast to the psychotic. [p. 105]

Nunberg makes what I consider a somewhat controversial point in relation to repression and its role in obsessional neurosis. After describing the regression to the anal-sadistic stage and how the "sexual impulses invade the consciousness again, only they are no longer genital but anal-sadistic in character," he continues: "Regression is no longer sufficient to ward them off, because it has already fulfilled its task once [in the regression from the phallic-oedipal phase to the anal-sadistic state], and neither is repression, *because it is able to ward off only impulses on the genital stage*. . . . Thus still another process of defense has to be put into action." (author's emphasis) (p. 238).

I think there is no doubt that repression is a favored mechanism of defense when the ego has to deal with phallic-oedipal conflicts and for this very reason repression is the essential mechanism of hysteria. It is very different to state as definitely as Nunberg does that repression is useless as a defense mechanism when dealing with prephallic impulses. Later he goes on to say:

> We have further seen that the mechanism of defense at the genital stage and after the establishment of the superego is different from that on earlier developmental stages. It seems that repression is the defensive response on the genital stage of development, whereas reaction formations seem to bear a special relation to the pregenital stages of organization.
>
> If repression proves to be too weak a protection, then there sets in regressively other, older defense mechanisms, such as projection, identification, repetition compulsion, and reaction formation. [p. 249]

He remarks, following Freud, that

> it seems that symptom formation is not always concluded with the countercathexis. If, for instance, the reaction formation of the compulsive neurotic no longer suffices to prevent the return of the repressed impulse, then the other auxiliary techniques appear, such as undoing and isolating, which take on the character of a ceremonial. [p. 282]

Nunberg considers the question of gratification of libidinal and aggressive impulses, comparing it in conversion hysterics, obsessionals, phobics, melancholics, and schizophrenics.

In conversion hysterics, libido and aggression are gratified simultaneously and there may be no guilt; in obsessionals the gratification of the libidinal and the aggressive impulses alternate as if in a compromise; in the phobics "the libido is scarcely gratified, but the feeling of guilt is gratified in the form of the need for punishment, as for instance through the restriction of personal freedom"; in melancholics he considers that "there is no gratification of libido, but only of aggression," while in schizophrenics "the gratification of either depends on the stage of development of the illness" (p. 282).

Nunberg considers that "the feeling of guilt is more tormenting and aggressive in obsessional neurosis than in hysteria," and partly because of it "one might assume that the feeling of guilt of the obsessional neurotic is rooted more in fear of punishment, and that of the hysteric in fear of the loss of love (p. 236). He thinks that "in both cases, the feeling of guilt would injure the narcissism of the ego; in obsessional neurosis, through the threat of destruction on the part of the ego; in obsessional neurosis, through the threat of destruction on the part of the super ego; in hysteria, through the threat of destruction or the loss of its protective power (as the ego idea)." He goes on to state that the superego of obsessionals "is far more intolerant and demanding and has a greater power over the ego" than is the case in hysteria. This is so because "with a strongly anal-sadistic disposition, an extremely severe and unloving superego develops" (p. 238).

When describing certain character changes as the reactions to the anal-sadistic strivings to which the obsessional neurotic has regressed in his instinctual life, he compares what happens in hysteria. He says:

Similar reactions also appear in hysteria, but they do not change the patient's character, since they apply only to a definite situation or to a specific object. The hysterical woman who, in her heart, hates her husband displays excessive affection and anxiousness about him; for others close to her, whom she does not hate she shows no excessive affection nor anxiousness. [p. 239]

Nunberg refers to Freud's very interesting comparison between hysterics and obsessionals and the role of the countercathexis in both processes, as well as the relationship between repression and regression and what he refers to as "external and internal countercathexis." He says:

The countercathexis is an integral part of the resistances against the re-emergence of warded-off instinctual strivings. Whereas, in hysteria, the resistance derived from the countercathexis serves mainly to reinforce the defense against external perceptions, its task, in obsessional neurosis, is exclusively to strengthen the defense against inner dangers, thus against the instincts themselves. In hysteria, the countercathexis is predominantly an external one; in obsessional neurosis, an internal one. To state it more clearly, the hysteric in the first place wards off his relationship to love objects; the obsessional neurotic wards off the instinct itself. The hysteric thereby breaks off the connection with consciousness, while the obsessional neurotic does not. Common to both is the fact that they ward off the undesirable perceptions and instinctual impulses through alteration of the ego organization. Since, in the obsessional neurosis, the decisive defense occurs through regression which forces the instinct life down to a lower level, and since, furthermore, the obsessional neurotic works against his instinct life with internal countercathexis, while the hysteric accomplishes the same with external countercathexis, it appears that there is a relationship between repression and internal countercathexis, on the other. [p. 244, see also Freud, 1926d, p. 159]

Finally, Nunberg compares obsessionals and hysterics in terms of the relation between body and psyche. In obsessionals,

the relation between body and psyche is looser. The symptoms have a more "psychic" character, the desires are not expressed by unconscious innervations of the body, but rather in voluntary, coordinated, usually very complicated actions, whose more or less conscious motive is caution or the wish to undo something. Between the driving forces of the id and the executive organ, the ego, a thought, a word, an idea is interpolated. There are even obsessional neuroses in which no compulsive action whatsoever takes place, and the entire process takes its course exclusively in "thoughts"; obsessional doubting is typical of this. The hysteric, on the other hand, has no "thoughts" since in the repression he has lost the verbal ideas, while in obsessional neurosis the verbal ideas have often been retained in consciousness. Most frequently they are merely "thoughts" which seem remote to the patient and yet are charged with affect. [pp. 286-287]

Fenichel in his book *The Psychoanalytic Theory of the Neurosis* (1945) has a specific chapter on obsessional neurosis. It is based largely on Freud's formulations, though interesting contributions by other authors are at times referred to.

Fenichel points out that the regression leads to enhanced sadism that "combines with the Oedipus hostility felt for the parent of the same sex and imposes new defensive tasks on the ego" (p. 277).

He remarks on the bisexual conflicts of the obsessional: "Anal eroticism, it has been stated, is always bisexual in nature, the anus being simultaneously an active expelling organ and a hollow organ which may be stimulated by some object entering it." Similarly:

Vacillation between the original masculine attitude, now reinforced and exaggerated by the active-sadistic component of anal eroticism, and the feminine attitude represented by the passive component of anal eroticism forms the most typical conflict in the unconscious of the male compulsion neurotic. The phallic Oedipus attitude is inhibited by the idea that gratification means the loss of the penis. The regression imposes a feminine attitude, yet does not entirely destroy the original masculine one.

The aim of the feminine wishes of male compulsion is not, of course, to be castrated; it is rather the wish for something to be inserted or retained in the body. [p. 277]

He notes the fact that "the morality demanded by the archaic superego of the compulsion neurotic is an automatized pseudo-morality, characterized by Alexander as the corruptibility of the superego."

In discussing the problem of the differential etiology in hysteria and obsessionals he states, as Freud did, that the basic conflict is the same in both, that is, the Oedipus complex. He remarks on the importance of the anal-sadistic regression in obsessionals and considers that this regression depends on one of three factors or their combinations.

The first is "the residuals of the anal-sadistic phase" in the personality. He thinks that "the outcome of the original anal-sadistic phase is probably the crucial factor." The regression is easier the greater the fixation at that stage. The latter can be caused by a) "constitutional factors"; b) "unusual gratifications"; c) "unusual frustrations"; d) "an alternation of unusual gratifications and unusual frustrations"; and e) "a concurrence of instinctual gratifications with reassurance against specific anxieties."

The second factor concerns the phallic organization and its "weakness." The existence of important pregenital fixations implies a weaker phallic organization.

The third factor refers to "the defending ego." He considers that

the ego that is especially apt to resort to the use of regression for defense is "strong" in one respect and "weak" in another. The critical function of the ego and the need for preparatory thinking must have developed especially early, certainly in the phase when the thinking functions were still magically oriented; but this very necessity for the defensive ego to start functioning so early causes the methods used to be archaic and immature ones. The ego of compulsion neurotics must be strong enough to enforce its protests against the instincts at a very early date, yet it must be too weak to fight out this conflict by more mature methods. In contrast, many persons who are inclined towards introverted daydreaming and who later develop conversion symptoms show a relative inhibition of their intellectual functions. [pp. 305-306]

He poses Freud's question as to the existence of compulsion neuroses not based on a regression from the phallic-oedipal phase but on disturbances in the anal-sadistic stage that prevented "the development of a full phallic Oedipus complex." He answers this by saying:

Cases of this kind do occur. However, they do not represent the typical compulsion neurosis. The great importance of the Oedipus complex, of castration anxiety, and of masturbation in the typical compulsion neurosis is well established. The disturbances of development during the anal-saidstic phase produce, rather, personalities without pronounced compulsive symptoms but with a character similar to that of compulsion neurotics, mixed with general infantile traits. [p. 306]

Fenichel considers that the "compulsion neuroses in adults fall into two groups: the rare acute forms and the more common chronic forms." The chronic type is the most frequent and is usually a continuation more or less without interruption from adolescence, though exacerbations occur from time to time (p. 306).

He considers that among the cases of compulsion neuroses some are stationary—the defenses being relatively successful—while others are "progressive." "In the latter, either 'breakdowns' of relative, compulsive equilibriums occur, with the open production of anxiety and depressions (which may be favorable for analysis), or there is a continuous increase of the compulsive symptoms toward the feared final states of full paralysis of the conscious will" (p. 307).

After remarking how in analysis the uncovering of the "anal-sadistic world" is followed by the recovery of the phallic memories shattered by the castration anxiety, Fenichel continues:

> It is important not to be misled into thinking that newly appearing memories with reference to anal-sadistic impulses are memories from the time of the original anal-sadistic organization. Very often they are not original but regressive in nature; they came after the phallic Oedipus complex; and the original pregenital organization must be dated still earlier. [p. 276]

Finally, Fenichel's remarks as to the difficulties presented by the treatment of obsessionals are pertinent here. He considers the analysis of obsessionals much more difficult than that of hysterics. He warns against promises of cure in severe cases, and points out that frequently one must be contented with only some measure of improvement.

He enumerates eight points as especially relevant in this context:

1. Obsessionals find it difficult if not impossible to comply with the basic rule. Fenichel says: "To find a way for the patient to learn what it feels like to associate freely, and at the same time to avoid holding theoretical discussions and furnishing him with new material for brooding, is perhaps the main technical task in the analysis of a compulsion neurotic" (p. 309).
2. The fact that portions of the ego think magically, not logically, taking side with the resistances and the role played by the superego makes the analysis especially difficult.
3. Because of the regression, analysis has to go deeper in obsessionals than in hysterics.
4. Because of the anal-sadistic regression, the object relationships are more difficult, governed by ambivalence and subbornness which will become manifest in the transference.
5. There is a tendency to isolate ideational content from emotions,

with the danger of an analysis remaining on the intellectual level only.

6. Thinking and talking (the instuments of psychoanalysis) are sexualized in the compulsion neurosis.
7. The nature of the secondary gain is integrally bound up in the personality of the obsessional, as is the narcisstic gain from the reaction-formations. Some "good" obsessionals do not accept what they feel as being "corrupted" by analysis. The analyst can be felt as a seducer.
8. The appearance of anxiety or its physical equivalents creates severe complications in persons who do not like affects and whose symptoms are in the "mental sphere only."

He concludes that though these difficulties are not insuperable they contribute to make analysis of obsessionals difficult and time-consuming (the notorious "long" analyses) (pp. 308-310).

Abraham has contributed several papers (1912, 1919, 1921, 1924) relevant to ceremonials, obsessional neurosis, and anal characters. He has compared certain aspects of melancholia and obsessional neurosis.

In his 1919 paper, "A Particular Form of Neurotic Resistance Against the Psychoanalytic Method," he describes how the analysis of obsessionals presents numerous difficulties. Fenichel's description above is no doubt partly based on this paper.

Abraham points to the particular difficulty experienced by obsessionals in regard to free associations. He says: "Whereas in most of our cases we meet with a resistance of this kind which appears and disappears by turns, there is a small group of neurotics who keep it up without interruption during the whole of their treatment. This chronic resistance to the fundamental rule of psychoanalysis may obstruct its progress very much and even preclude a successful result." Abraham goes on to explain that these patients do not say that "nothing occurs" to them; on the contrary they speak in a continuous, unbroken manner and resent being interrupted. Nevertheless, they are not free-associating but rather talking according to a program. They arrange what they have to say "according to central lines of thought and subject it to extensive criticism and modification on the part of the ego" (pp. 303-304).

These patients can in fact be very deceptive to the analyst if he does not recognize this specific form of resistance . . . because they seem willing and "their communications are superabundant in quantity," but they say only things that are ego syntonic (p. 305).

Abraham describes in the paper several other characteristics of these obsessional patients such as the unmistakable element of "envy." The analyst must not supply anything to the treatment because the patient wants to do everything himself. They tend to make up at home for the failure to associate freely during the session. They do "autoanalysis" at home and present the analyst with their "gift," in this way showing the revolt against the father (pp. 307-308).

Their parsimony does not contradict the fact that these patients are ready to make material sacrifices for their treatment since by so doing, they make "a sacrifice to their narcissism." Their parsimony is expressed in their saving up their unconscious material. "They practice constipation in their psychoanalysis, just as they do in the sphere of bowel activity" (p. 310).

In his paper "A Short Study of the Libido Viewed in the Light of Mental Disorders" (1924), Abraham makes a number of interesting comparisons between obsessionals and melancholics. He remarks for example on the psychological affinity between melancholia and obsessional neurosis, in that both show disengagement of the libido from the external world. An important difference is that while the melancholic loses his object before the outbreak of the illness, the obsessional neurotic has a "markedly ambivalent attitude toward his object and is afraid of losing it but he does ultimately keep it."

In pointing to the resemblances between the two illnesses (melancholia and obsessional neurosis), Abraham remarks that there are not only resemblances in the acute symptoms but also during the periods of quiescence. While manic-depressive states run an intermittent course and obsessional states are on the whole chronic in character, the latter also show tendencies toward considerable remission. Furthermore,

in all cycloid illnesses the patient is found to have an abnormal character-formation during his "free interval"; and this character-formation coincides in a quite unmistakable way with that of the obsessional neurotic. . . . In their "free interval" patients suffering from circular insanity exhibit the same characteristics as psychoanalysis has made us acquainted with in the obsessional neuroses— the same peculiarities in regard to cleanliness and order; the same tendency to take up an obstinate and defiant attitude alternating with exaggerated docility and an excess of "goodness"; the same abnormalities of behavior in relation to money and possessions.

He refers to the two levels of the anal-sadistic stage, saying: "On the later level the conserving tendencies of retaining and controlling the object predominate, whereas on the earlier level those hostile to their object—those of destroying and losing it—come to the fore. The obsessional neurotic regresses to the later of these two levels, and so he is able to maintain contact with his object."

Abraham's concern for the study of the similarities and differences between obsessionals and melancholics was of long standing. When, partly in reaction to an earlier paper by Abraham Freud wrote his essay "Mourning and Melancholia" (1917e), he sent it to Abraham with a request for comments. The latter was especially concerned to ascertain the psychological differences between obsessionals and melancholics, because these two conditions have otherwise so much in common. He "suggested that although sadism was important in both, the oral factor played the part in melancholia that anal erotism does in obsessional neurosis." According to Jones (1955), Freud replied: "Your comments on Melancholia I found very valuable. I have unhesitatingly incorporated in my essay what I found useful. The most valuable point was your remark about the oral phase of the libido . . ." (p. 368).

Alexander in his book *Fundamentals of Psychoanalysis* (1948) describes the two sides of the personality of the obsessional. He considers that "the obsessional symptom represents a breach in the repressive defenses through which alien wishes emerge." He continues:

By isolating them from the rest of his personality the patient does not feel them to be his own and assumes no responsibility for them. Thus assertion of the most frankly asocial tendencies in conscious fantasies is made possible by a mechanism described as bribing the superego. The compulsive patient is hypermoralistic, exceptionally clean, punctilious or truthful, industrious, meticulous, and conventional. He overdoes all this and can therefore allow himself to indulge in prohibited phantasies. These two sides of his personality, the "good" and the "bad," social and asocial, clean and dirty, hostile and considerate, are in a constant struggle with each other, and the whole neurosis consists in preserving their equilibrium. [p. 220]

Barnett (1966) describes "certain cognitive disorders in the obsessional that appear to be core phenomena, more central to the obsessional way of living than has been considered heretofore" (p. 122). Further, he views "the obsessional as a markedly ineffectual thinker. The much vaunted thinking ability of the obsessional appears to be a myth without foundation in clinical reality. Imagery is limited, novelty and originality are sacrificed to rigidity of thought, cliche, and endless elaboration of detail. Spontaneity, novelty, and creativity are minimal. Blocking of thought processes, sterotype, perserveration, and detailed, unimaginative use of language, all underscore the fact of the obsessional's difficulty in thinking. . . . He seems doomed to travel the most circuitous route in the development of a thought" (p. 124).

In a later paper Barnett (1969) noted that "few clinical conditions serve as well for a study of aggression in its many expressions as do the obsessional neuroses." Among other things, he discusses some forms the expression of hostility takes in the obsessional, such as defiance or such covert forms of defiance as certain types of inhibition. Further, he makes the interesting suggestion that the severity of guilt in obsessionals may be due rather to a *defect* of conscience than to the more usually assumed *severity* of conscience.

Blacker (1966) has wondered specifically about the relationship between obsessional neuroses and catatonia. He conceives "of these two disorders as representing points on a continuum, catatonia being viewed as the extreme form" (p. 191). In the same paper he refers not only to a case of his own but to other cases in the literature that he thinks support his contention of catatonia "as the primitive end point of obsessive-compulsive defenses" (p. 185).

Chethik (1969), in describing the treatment of a latency child suffering from an obsessional neurosis, tells how the treatment faced the same difficult tasks described by Fenichel in regard to similar conditions in adults. Hence the difficulties with free association, the tendency to intellectualized brooding, the magical thinking that interferes with the ego's capacity for observation, the excessive use of isolation, etc. He says: "All the above *tendencies* were evident in the work with Fred, but one senses from this experience the enormous advantages when analysis begins relatively early in the patient's life" (p. 481).

According to Chethik, Fred's affects (in spite of the tendency to isolation) seemed more readily available since they were not yet totally buried by multiple layers of defenses (as would be the case with adults). Fred, too, made his analyst an object for the externalization of his inner conflicts. Obsessional children, like children in general, tend, in my own experience, to greatly favor the use of externalization side by side with the more traditional obsessional defenses. I can confirm too from personal experience Chethik's distinct impression that in well-established obsessional neurosis in children other forms of psychopathology are significantly present, frequently conveying the impression of a "mixed neurosis" though they are distinctly obsessional (pp. 481-482).

Ferenczi (1913), writing about adult obsessional patients, has the following to say:

> The obsessional neurosis constitutes a relapse of the mental life to that stage of child development characterized, amongst other things, by there being as yet no inhibiting, postponing, reflecting thought-activity interposed between wishing and acting, the wish-fulfilling movement following spontaneously and unhesitatingly on the wishing—an averting movement away from something disagreeable, or an approach towards something agreeable. A part of the mental life, more or less removed from consciousness, thus remains with the obsessional patient . . . on this childhood level in consequence of an arrest in development (fixation) and makes wishing equivalent to acting because . . . this repressed portion of the mental life was not able to learn the difference between the two activities. . . .

Anna Freud in *The Ego and the Mechanisms of Defence* (1937) says that "in obsessional neurosis, as in hysteria, hatred of the mother and penis-envy are in the first instance repressed. Subsequently the ego secures itself against their return by means of reaction-formations."

In her later book, *Normality and Pathology in Childhood, Assessments of Development* (1965), Anna Freud has referred to the fact that "a close correspondence has been shown repeatedly between the manifest symptomatology of the infantile and adult neuroses. . . . On the side of the *obsessional* neurosis, both children and adults show the painfully heightened ambivalence of feeling, the bedtime ceremonials, other rituals, washing compulsions, repetitive actions, questions, formulas; magic words and gestures, or magic avoidance of particular words and movements; compulsions to count and list; to touch or avoid touch, etc." She further points out that in some cases "the step from hysterical to obsessional symptomatology" is linked with maturational processes of the ego which is why". . . defenses against anxiety which make use of the motor system such as bodily conversion and phobic retreat, change to defense mechanisms within the thought processes such as counting, magical formulas, undoing, isolating. . . ." She thinks that well-organizaed obsessional manifestations in very young children have "to be understood probably as early ominous signs of splits and disharmonies within the structure, severe enough to lead later to a psychotic total disintegration of the personality." Finally she refers to a transitory obsessional phase which appears in the majority of children "around or after the height of the anal phase." It can create a misleading picture of pathology when in fact "the compulsive manifestations disappear without trace as soon as the relevant drive and ego positions have been outgrown."

While discussing the question of uneven drive and ego progression she says:

> We expect pathological consequences to follow in cases where development proceeds at different speeds in different areas of the personality. One of these eventualities, with which we are familiar, forms part of the etiology of the obsessional neurosis where ego and superego development are accelerated while drive development is slowed up, or at least is slow in comparison with it. The incompatibility between relatively high moral and aesthetic superego demands and relatively crude fantasies and drive

derivatives leads to the internal conflict by which in turn the obsessional defense activity is set in motion.

She discusses the question of regression and permanent regressions, and points to children "whose ego agencies are strong enough to resist regression." In these cases a variety of different symptoms or character traits may develop "according to the specific drive elements to which they object most strongly." She continues:

Where the dirty, the sadistic and the passive trends are rejected by ego and superego with equal intensity, the defense is spread over the whole field and the symptomatology is profuse. Where only one or the other is singled out, the symptoms will be restricted to either excessive cleanliness, pollution fears, washing compulsions, or inhibition of activity and competition, or fears of being turned into a female, or compensatory outbursts of aggressive masculinity, etc. In any case, the result is unmistakably *neurotic,* whether in the form of isolated obsessional symptoms or the beginning of obsessional character formation. [p. 51, see also A. Freud, 1965]

The purpose of Gelfman's paper (1970) is to "attempt an expression of the obsessive-compulsive characterological systems of value (consciousness) and especially to delineate certain irresponsible qualities of this structure" (p. 37).

His definition of obsessional neurosis is at great variance with the traditional one. He sees the obsessive patient's need for excessive control as actually that of "an individual who 'fears' a loss of control . . . because he is most anxious to avoid a situation where he may be responsible to or answerable to a person, situation, or force outside himself" (p. 39). In a similar vein he approaches the disorders of thinking, the need for perfectionism, as well as the role of suppressed hostility in obsessionals. He concludes that the obsessional "chooses to be a power of influence and control over others by manufacturing inauthentic traits of excellence" (p. 46).

Gero and Rubenfine in their paper "Obsessive Thoughts" (1955) discuss mainly the case history of an obsessional with numerous obsessive thoughts, one of which was an obsessive fear of killing a child. In relation to the mechanism of symptom formation they have the following to say:

To understand symptom formation in obsessive neurosis an important statement of Freud has to be remembered, namely that repression is a mobile process. The term "mobility of repression" indicates that parts of the sexual drives and phantiasies underlying the obsessive symptom are consciously perceived at times. ... Whenever an obsessive symptom is formed, the partial repression, which allowed limited discharge in phantasies and masturbatory activities, is replaced by total repression. As libidinal cathexes is completely withdrawn, the sexual character of the symptom is not recognizable to our patients. At the same time object-directed phantasies are transformed into narcissistic ones, and object relations are replaced by identifications. ... Total repression is the answer to stimuli which reactivate the unconscious oedipal phantasies and with them genital anxieties and superego prohibitions.

In his paper "A Developmental Study of the Obsessional Neuroses" (1935) Glover suggests that in order fully to understand the etiology of obsessional neurosis, its relation both to hysteria and the psychoses must be considered. In point of fact, "the degree of ramification of a neurosis is itself significant. The more extensively a symptom-construction is spread over or penetrates ego-structure, the more likely is it to correspond to a phase of ego development. In other words, the complexity of the obsessional neurosis is a tribute to the scope, vigor and elasticity of its defensive functions." One of the prime tasks of obsessional neurosis "is to permit a regressive flight from the anxieties induced by advancing development, and at the same time to stem that regression." In adult cases, "clinical examination shows how frequently behind the constructions of anxiety hysteria there appear layers of obsessional organization. When the hysterical defense fails to stem regression this obsessional layer is ready to take up the additional burden."

Glover is in part concerned in this paper with the developmental and defensive functions of obsessional mechanisms and symptoms. He puts the phase of "obsessional primacy" in the infant at roughly between eighteen months and three and one-half years and says: "Whereas the obsessional neurosis [in adults] serves to conceal the fact that, but for its help in instinctual crises, there would be no stopping place for the patient short of the psychoses, the 'obsessional phase' of infancy serves to conceal the fact that but for its activities there would never by any advance for any child out of the 'normal pan-psychosis' of the first year."

He proposes in general that one should examine two specific factors in symptom formation: "a) certain more or less stable combinations of endo-psychic factors; and b) environmental stimuli, if any, associated *exclusively* with the particular form of neurosis under investigation."

In considering the specific mechanism exploited in obsessional neurosis, Glover remarks on the importance of displacement:

> Studying the clinical features of various obsessions, it is easy to draw a working distinction between ideational, speech and behavioristic end-products. These products can then be subdivided quite elaborately in accordance with the amount of *psychic distance* interposed between instinct derivatives and their possible expression in action. . . . Speaking broadly, the content of ideational obsessions can be arranged in an ascending series: viz. aggressive images, sexual images, images concerning matters of social importance to the individual, images concerning social matters of trivial order and more or less nonsensical images. That is to say, however much an apparently nonsensical obsession may give indirect expression to instinct through the processes of symbolism, condensation and distortion, the practical fact remains that direct expression is minimal. The obsession is a widely displaced derivative. In the ritual (behavioristic) obsessions a similar arrangement can be detected. Nonsensical or trivial expressions are most frequent, whilst social rituals, in the sense of compulsive sexual or aggressive acts, are least frequent. Comparing these two types, it is evident that much more direct expression of instinct is permitted in the ideational obsession that in the obsessional action. [With regard to word obsessions,] more latitude appears to be allowed to obscene and aggressive words than is the case with the two other types described.

Furthermore, each of these obsessions (ideational, behavioristic and speech) has a "positive and negative phase." "The ideational obsession is accompanied or alternates with phases of doubt and rumination; obsessional actions are associated with fluctuating phases of abulia (indecision), whilst word obsessions are frequently accompanied by difficulty in verbal expression."

Disturbances of affect are of three main types: "reactions of guilt associated with 'forbidden' thoughts and actions; reactions of anxiety or panic when expiatory or protective rituals are neglected; and a degree of emotional impoverishment." Glover also suggests, on the basis of clinical observations, that "what we usually term clinical obsessional neuroses, with their elaborate thought, speech and action rituals, are really in the neurotic sense highly sophisticated end-products. The primary obsessional state is essentially an affective state or rather a sequence of alternating affects having very simple ideational content."

Considering obsessional neuroses where the obsessive content in the main deals with affective experiences ("emotional obsessions"), Glover states that he was able "to detect simply and well-defined anxieties about the body, its integrity and its relation to the bodies of objects, in short, the now familiar systems of body-phantasy." The conclusion he draws is that "the main function of the obsessional system must be to combine and consolidate the advantages of introjection and projection mechanisms and at the same time to eliminate as far as possible the disadvantages of depending too exclusively on any one mechanism. . . . The function of the obsessional neurosis is not only to split up mental tensions before they reach the stage of producing panic and to allow a more rapid swing between introjection and projection affects, but by expanding the mechanism of displacement, to develop the first stable relation between the ego and its objects. In other words, obsessional mechanisms soften the sharpness of introjections, prevent irrevocable projections and, by their flexible range of intercommunication, bind the ego to the object."

Finally, Glover inquires into the relation between obsessional symptoms and anxiety phobias. He suggests that "the connection between anxiety-phobias, obsessions and fears of a projection type is much closer than the clinical features suggest."

In his book *The Technique of Psycho-Analysis* (1955) Glover, besides describing a number of interesting technical questions regarding the treatment of obsessionalsm makes the following points of theoretical interest. He refers to the typical "touching taboo" of the obsessional and how it is frequently intended to counteract masturbatory impulses (p. 116; see also Glover, 1939).

He talks about "mixed neurosis," that is, obsessional neurosis that is not "pure" but a mixture of hysteria and obsessional neurosis. According to him this type is by far the most accessible variety of obsessional. The obsessional system is set in them "in a matrix of hysterical formations." He claims that they show "that the distinction between the hysterias and obsessional neuroses is not so clear-cut as the classical clinical symptoms would suggest" (pp. 190-191).

Prognostically he considers "major obsessional neurosis" as "a severe and intractable disorder in which only moderate analytical accessibility prevails." He points out that frequently the obsessional neurosis acts as a defensive cover for "depressive or persecutory substructures" (p. 205).

He believes "that the obsessional neuroses date in most instances from about the age of two years, that they constitute a pathological overemphasis of a normal obsessional phase, that this normal phase is intended to consolidate ego development and render the ego less sensitive to violent alterations of projective and intrjective phases" (p. 368).

Greenacre's paper "A Study of the Mechanism of Obsessive-Compulsive Conditions" (1922-23) seems to date from her preanalytic times. She studied eighty-six patients and stated that they first came for treatment at some point between the ages of sixteen and forty. Acute symptoms began most frequently between the ages of twenty-one and twenty-five, but commonly the patients gave a retrospective account of obsessions and compulsions beginning before puberty.

She posed three questions: (1) Are phobias, obsessions and compulsions common in childhood? (2) When they occur, do those of normal children differ from the manifestations of the potential obsessional? (3) What is the significance of any differences? She studied thirty normal people and found that twenty-nine recalled some phobia, obsession, or compulsion in childhood though none in this group had become psychoneurotic.

The content of these more normal phobias and compulsions was on the whole different from the childhood phobias of potential patients.

Many (normal compulsions) were indulged by groups of children and
were incorporated in their play activity, such as the step-on-a-crack
prohibition: "Step on a crack, break your mother's back!"

She shows "three stages in the development of a profound obsessive-
compulsion or phobic condition" as combinations of the balancing of a
wish with the fear of the consequences (p. 527).

Hartmann in 1933 investigated the question of the remembering or
recall of completed and uncompleted activities in obsessional neurosis.
He said:

> For several reasons, it seemed to me of interest to investigate the
> behavior of obsessive-compulsive neurotics with respect to this
> question. Various authors have correctly emphasized that incom-
> pleteness or inability of closure is characteristic of the thinking of
> obsessive-compulsive neurotics. This quality of their thought
> processes in particular gave rise to the expectation that the "tensions
> systems" might in their case act differently from the way in which
> they act in normals, and that this difference might be verified
> experimentally. Thus some light might be thrown also on the
> tendency toward repetition, which is a well-known but not yet fully
> understood characteristic of obsessional neurosis.

His findings show, in contradistinction to those by Zeigarnik to
which he refers, that "obsessive-compulsive neurotics recall uncompleted activities *hardly* better than completed ones."

Nonetheless, Hartmann does not regard his results as especially
significant and, agreeing with further observations made by Zeigarnik,
he emphasizes that "subjective incompletion of a task and the tendency
for repetition must be recognized as influences upon recall." He goes
on to inquire what the situation is concerning this "need to repeat" in
his obsessional subjects. He reviews the various aspects of compulsive
repetitions in obsessional neurosis—i.e. diphasic symptoms, belief in
the magical omnipotence of thought, inhibition of thought, undoing
and repeating—and then elaborates on this obsession to repeat:

> The repetition is aimed at weakening or cancelling the magical
> significance of an action. If, however, the obsessive-compulsive
> neurotic's strict superego was not satisfied with the details of the

repetition, then further repetitions follow. The magical world of the obsessional neurotic and his hypercathexis of thought processes—which are related to his typical regression and to the restriction of his activities (activity equals destruction)—also are responsible for his endeavor to blur the differences between what actually happened and what possibly might have happened, between what has been done and what has been thought. Now we understand why, for the obsessive-compulsive neurotic, the character of "completeness" of an action remains subjectively relative, and where the "need to repeat" originates. This is also the source to which the peculiarity of the results obtained with the obsessive-compulsive subjects can be attributed. Here we see the factors which find their expression in the altered structure of their "quasi needs."

Hartmann (1950) has emphasized the need to replace such terms as "'precocious' or 'retarded ego development' by more detailed statements specifying what ego functions have actually undergone a precocious or retarded development in relation to the drives and in relation to one another." He thinks that when we speak of "precocious ego development, as in the pathogeny of obsessional neuroses, actually only the intellectual or the defensive functions of the ego have prematurely developed, while, for instance, the tolerance for unpleasure is retarded." In the same paper he remarks that "characteristics of a certain phase may occasionally appear earlier [because of deviations in the timing of the typical phases]; that is, before the main elements of the phase to which we are used to relate these features have become dominant. . . . Reaction formations, like orderliness or cleanliness, displacements, generalized attitudes, which we are accustomed to find correlated with the anal phase, may then appear before problems of anality have come to dominate the child's life" (pp. 107, 109).

Hoffer in *Psychoanalysis: Practical and Research Aspects* (1955), while discussing the different sources of anxiety in the human being, points out the fear of one's conscience and of feeling guilty. He thinks obsessionals are excellent examples of this phenomenon: "One need only study obsessional neurotics to see superego anxiety, anxiety of the conscience at work, if one has any doubt about it" (p. 34).

Historically speaking, it was Ernest Jones (1923) who first drew attention to the relationship between anal erotism and cruelty. He said:

In the obsessional neurosis the association between hate and anal erotism is certainly very frequent [as at the stage where the infant finds itself in serious conflict with the external world for the first time—i.e. during toilet training] being in my experience a constant occurence.... As is now known, the chief characteristic in the psychology of the neurosis is the mutual paralysis of the tendencies of love and hate, with the resulting alternation of compulsion and doubt. This curious phenomenon becomes more intelligible when we remember that the hate, according to my view, is first developed toward the imago of all later love objects, the mother herself; thus the capacity to love is impeded or paralysed at its very inception. It is only to be expected that any one whose love towards the mother has from the beginning alternated with hate should show the same alternation towards all secondary love-objects.

Jones suggests that there is a higher incidence of obsessional neurosis in men, in that the boy's hate of the mother in the anal stage complicates the subsequent oedipal involvement, whereas with the girl it merely anticipates it.

Defiance toward a person of greater strength, which is a concomitant of hate, is an attitude always found in the obsessional neurosis, where it is transferred onto the father.

The obsessional neurotic's "inordinate belief in the omnipotence of his thoughts" (his sense of power) is linked by Jones to a statement of Ferenczi's: "I would relate the sense of compulsion in the obsessional neurosis, one which in its genesis is closely connected with the feeling of omnipotence, in part to the overpowering force with which an anal-erotic desire may present itself."

Kayton and Borge (1967) after acknowledging the unreliability of correlation studies between psychopathology and ordinal position, studied the chart of forty patients from an outpatient psychiatric clinic. Their hypothesis was that firstborn and only children would be overrepresented in the obsessive-compulsive character disorder because such ordinal positions may foster premature ego development. This is in line, they thought, with the psychoanalytic hypothesis that precocious ego development may be a significant factor in the development of obsessional difficulties.

They found that thirty-one of the forty obsessive-compulsives were first-born or only children, compared to eleven of forty in the control group. They concluded that "in this population, the obsessive-compulsive character disorder occurs predominately in males who are either firstborn or only children."

Melanie Klein's views have to be considered in two stages: before her description of the "paranoid and depressive position" and afterwards. Nevertheless the period before the formulation of the "paranoid and depressive positions" contains in an abridged form many of the essentials of her later formulations.

The first period is perhaps best represented in her book *The Psychoanalysis of Children* (1932), in which she connects obsessional neurosis and psychosis:

> The process of modification of a phobia is, I believe, linked with those mechanisms upon which the obsessional neuroses are based and which begin to be active in the later stage. It seems to me that obsessional neurosis is an attempt to cure the psychotic conditions which underlie it, and that in infantile neuroses both obsessional mechanisms and mechanisms belonging to a previous stage of development are already operative.

She continues:

> At first glance it would seem that this idea that certain elements of obsessional neurosis play an important role in the clinical picture presented by infantile neuroses is at variance with what Freud has said concerning the starting point of obsessional neurosis. Nevertheless, I believe that the disagreement can be explained away in one important point at least. It is true that according to my findings the origins of obsessional neurosis lie in the first period of childhood; but the isolated obsessional traits which emerge in that period are not organized into that whole which we regard as an obsessional neurosis until the second period of childhood, that is, until the beginning of the latency period. The accepted theory is that fixations at the anal-sadistic stage do not come into force as factors

in obsessional neurosis until later on, as the result of a regression to them. My view is that the true point of departure for obsessional neurosis—the point at which the child develops obsessional symptoms and obsessional mechanisms—is situated in that period of life which is governed by the later anal stage. The fact that this early obsessional illness presents a somewhat different picutre from the later full-blown obsessional neurosis is understandable if we recollect that it is not until late, in the latency period, that the more mature ego, with its altered relationship to reality, sets to work to elaborate and synthesize those obsessional features which have been active since early childhood. [pp. 226-227]

Her argument at this point is based on a discussion of what she thinks are the differences between her formulations and those of Freud. Some of these arguments seem to suggest her having overlooked some of Freud's formulations. For example, she states above that "the accepted theory is that fixations at the anal-sadistic stage do not come into force as factors in obsessional neurosis until later on, as the result of regression to them." This is, I think, an incorrect assessment on her part of Freud's view as to the role played by the anal-sadistic fixation in the later obsessional developments, as we hope our review of Freud's formulation in Chapter 1 has made abundantly clear. Furthermore, in his paper "The Disposition to Obsessional Neurosis" (1913i) Freud distinguished between two possible types of development in obsessional neurosis. The first has its onset at an early age and then runs a chronic course with exacerbations at different times. In this group, "once the sexual organization [anal-sadistic stage] which contains the disposition to obsessional neurosis is established it is never afterwards completely surmounted. . . ." The second type proceeds to a higher stage from whence there is a regressive move at a later time (p. 322).

She refers to one of her cases, Rita (two years, nine months of age) in order to show that "even quite young children frequently exhibit symptoms of a distinctly obsessional type, and there exist infantile neuroses in which a true obsessional neurosis already dominates the picture" (1932, p. 227). She continues: "When this is the case it means that the early anxiety situations are too powerful and have not been sufficiently modified and that the obsessional neurosis is a very grave one" (p. 228).

Trying to close the gap which she thinks exists between her views and those of Freud, she says: "In thus distinguishing between the early emergence of single obsessional traits and, later, true obsessional neuroses, I have, I hope, been able to bring the view put forward here concerning the genesis of obsessional neurosis more into line with the accepted theory" (p. 228).

And: "These objections would in part be overcome if we adopt the view put forward here that obsessional neurosis has its point of departure in the first period of childhood but does not set in in its full form till the beginning of the latency period" (p. 229).

She considers the existence of early obsessional mechanisms as proof of early superego development:

> The view that obsessional mechanisms begin to come into action very early in childhood, towards the end of the second year, is part of my general thesis that the superego is formed in the earliest stages of the child's life, being first felt by the ego as anxiety and then, as the early anal-sadistic stage gradually comes to a close, as a sense of guilt as well. . . . My contention that obsessional neurosis is a means of modifying early anxiety situations and that the severe superego which figures in it is no other than the unmodified, terrifying superego belonging to early stages of the child's development, brings us, I think, nearer to a solution of the problem of why the superego should in fact be such a severe one in this neurosis. [p. 229]

Similarly:

> If I am correct in my view that the magnitude and intensity of obsessional activities and the severity of the neurosis are equivalent to the extent and character of the anxiety arising from the earliest danger-situations, we shall be in a better position to understand the close connection which we know to exist between paranoia and the severer forms of obsessional neurosis. According to Abraham, in paranoia the libido regresses to the earlier of the two anal-sadistic stages. From what I have been able to discover I should be inclined to go further and say that in the early anal-sadistic stage the individual, if his early anxiety-situations are strongly operative,

actually passes through rudimentary paranoid states which he normally overcomes in the next stage (the second anal-sadistic one), and that the severity of his obsessional illness depends on the severity of the paranoid disturbances that have immediately preceded it. If his obsessional mechanisms cannot adequately overcome those disturbances his underlying paranoid traits will come to the surface, or he may even succumb to a regular paranoia. [pp. 232-233]

In her paper "A Contribution to the Theory of Intellectual Inhibition" (1931) she makes similar statements:

Let me say that in my view, as I shall shortly set out in detail, obsessional mechanisms and symptoms in general serve the purpose of binding, modifying and warding off anxiety belonging to the earliest levels of the mind; so that obsessional neuroses are built up upon the anxiety of the first danger-situations.

To return to the point: I think that the child's compulsive, almost greedy, collection and accumulation of things (including knowledge as a substance) is based, among other factors which need not be mentioned here, upon its ever-renewed attempt (1) to get hold of "good" substances and objects (ultimately, "good" milk, "good" faeces, a "good" penis and "good" children) and with their help to paralyze the action of the "bad" objects and substances inside its body; and (b) to amass sufficient reserves inside itself to be able to resist attack made upon it by its external objects, and if necessary to restore to its mother's body, or rather, to its objects, what it has stolen from them. Since its endeavours to do this by means of obsessional actions are continually being disturbed by onsets of anxiety from many countersources (for instance, its doubt whether what it has just taken into itself is really "good" and whether what it has cast out was really the "bad" part of its inside; or its fear that in putting more material into itself it has once more been guilty of robbing its mother's body) we can understand why it is under a constant obligation to repeat its attempts and how that obligation is in part responsible for the compulsive character of its behavior. [p. 265]

In "Mourning and Its Relation to Manic-Depressive States" (1940):

I have described elsewhere my conclusions that the obsessional mechanisms are a defense against paranoid anxieties as well as a means of modifying them, and here I will only show briefly the connection between obsessional mechanisms and manic defenses in relation to the depressive position in normal development. [p. 318]

She adds: "As a result of the failure of the act of reparation, the ego has to resort again and again to obsessional and manic defenses" (p. 318). Mrs. Klein has given, as a factor "of the greatest importance in the development of obsessional neurosis generally," the "feeling of guilt engendered by the superego" (1927, p. 194).

In the paper "Notes on Some Schizoid Mechanisms" (1946) she remarks:

The impulse to control other people is, as we know, an essential element in obsessional neurosis. The need to control others can to some extent be explained by a deflected drive to control parts of the self. When these parts have been projected excessively into another person, they can only be controlled by controlling the other person. One root of obsessional mechanisms may thus be found in the particular identification which results from infantile projective processes. [p. 306]

Finally, in her paper "Some Theoretical Conclusions Regarding the Emotional Life of the Infant" (1952), she says:

Obsessional mechanisms form an important part of ego-development. They enable the ego to keep anxiety temporarily at bay. This in turn helps the ego to achieve greater integration and strength; thereby the gradual working through, diminishing and modifying of anxiety become possible. However, obsessional mechanisms are only one of the defenses at this stage. If they are excessive and become the main defence, this can be taken as an indication that the ego cannot effectively deal with anxiety of a psychotic nature and that a sever obsessional neurosis is developing in the child. [p. 227]

Kline (1967) verified the validity of the dichotomy obsessional traits versus symptoms, thus confirming the psychoanalytic tenet that traits represent a successful ego defense while signs and symptoms are evidence of the breakdown in the defensive system.

Kline (1968) sudied the relationship between obsessional characteristics and toilet training, concluding that toilet training is only one factor in the etiology, the other and no less important being the constitution of the individual. This, in his view, possibly explains the failure to find support for the theory relating toilet training to anal characteristics, since such over-simplifications ignore the similarly significant constitutional factors. In this study, correlations "between the objective measures of obsessionality and anal erotism were in the expected direction and Freudian theory was regarded as supported."

Kringlen (1970) has approached the natural history of obsessional neurosis, reviewing the field and following ninety-one patients herself. She points out the innumerable methodological problems that arise in such a study; these coupled with the scarcity of follow-up studies and the disparity of the samples and procedures, made any conclusions quite tentative.

Her main findings (according to her Oslo sample) were as follows:

1. Obsessional neuroses have a relatively early onset of symptoms and a poor prognosis with few long remissions and few improvements.
2. Their enjoyment of life is poor and about three fourths of the sample were essentially unchanged at the time of follow-up (with a mean of thirty years).
3. Obsessionals tend to carry the burden of their illness by themselves. They are not inclined to seek medical treatment.
4. Though the spontaneous course of the illness is discouraging, they have on the whole rather stable personalities.
5. The question of how many of them become psychotic remains unsettled, but at least according to Stengel (quoted by Kringlen) relatively few do so. She herself thinks this is rare in typical cases.
6. Suicidal risk is very small.
7. Though misuse of alcohol and drugs can be found, actual alcoholism or drug addition is rare among them.

Bertram D. Lewin in his paper "Obsessional Neuroses" (1948) distinuishes two types of compulsive phenomena: (1) pointless and absurd ideas repugnant to the patient's moral and aesthetic feelings; and (2) acts representing penances, atonements, punishments— ordinary activities which have become elaborated into highly complicated rituals.

The patient is fequently aware of the content of the obsession; however, this manifest conetent serves to distort, through displacement and condensation, the latent meaning of the obsession. Obsessional ideas are representative of id infantile wishes. Obsessional acts emanate from unconscious superego commands—"a compulsion to wash certain parts of the body a certain number of times, orginally designed to ward off masturbatory impulses, may at the same time be a substitutive masturbation (i.e. accompanied by erotic thoughts, conscious or unconscious); or a moral compulsion may directly follow or precede one of the opposite type. It is apparently the object of the compulsion neurotic to attempt a sort of balance, quantitatively equalizing the extent to which he gives in to the primitive side and the moral side of his total personality."

Because the patient attributes a supersitious quality or sense of magic to external events he has repressed the internal relation between psychic events, and perceives them as external relations projected onto the external world. The child, the primitive and the obsessional neurotic share the same characteristic—that of overestimating the effect which either their love or hate can produce on the environment.

He points to the existence of many cases of "mixed neurosis," in which compulsive symptoms occur along side the phobic and hysterical, and to the fact that compulsive phenomena can be observed as well in manic-depressive psychosis and schizophrenia. As regards the onset of the illness, Lewin states that while compulsive phenomena may occur in the third year, the neurosis usually begins in the latency period, between the fourth and twelfth years.

Loewenstein (1945), while referring to some special forms of self-punishment, remarks that an analogous mechanism (the tranformation of the crime into self-punishment) is often observed in cases of compulsion neurosis in which the patient suffers from the obsessional fear of doing involuntary harm to someone, or from fear of the death of a near friend or relative, or from compulsive masturbation. "In all of these the repressed aggressive or sexual drives reappear in the symptom, and because of the repression the symptom is felt no longer as something to be desired but as something to be dreaded." Lowenstein likens this mechanism of transforming the crime into self-punishment to the diphasic character of compulsive symptoms, where the second phase contains the respressive and self-punishing forces.

Sandor Lorand in his paper "Compulsion Neurosis" (1947) says that because of the ambivalence, obsessional neurotics invariably present bizarre and contradictory symptoms. Such constant shifts in feelings make it difficult for analysts to maintain empathy. He points out that while regression to the anal stage results in strong ambivalence and narcissistic involvement, overlapping drives belonging to the oedipal phase are also present. He considers the symptom complex the result of compromise between instinctual drives and superego commands and prohibitions.

His main points can be summarized as follows:

Obsessions and compulsions are to be understood in the light of the patient's developmental history, where this is recoverable.

There is constant vacillation and indecision in the compulsion neurosis in regard to growing up or remaining a child; realizing genital tendencies or regressing to anal drives. The conflict ends in a compromise of partial regression to the anal-sadistic level, attempting thus to maintain some genital aims, while clinging at the same time to passive anal tendencies. Further complications arise from this compromise because implicit in the genital aims is the danger of castration. . . .

The severe self-punishing tendencies which so strongly interfere with the therapeutic process are a result of repressed aggression. It becomes evident in analysis that the anal activities and functions are charged with erotic feelings and, to a certain degree, carry genital aims. The superego, which is intolerant of genital desires, punishes anal activities because they satisfy sexual feelings. . . .

The patient's constant struggle is between his compulsive drives and self-condemnation for giving in to them. . . . The oedipal desires, which contain genital involvement, are fraught with danger for the ego. Therefore, regression to the anal phase of development is continually attempted. Feelings of rivalry and aggression, and desires to destroy the severe superego exist side by side with their opposites: desire for protection, guidance, love, reparation by the parents, who even though thought of as frustrating, demanding persons, are at the same time the objects of love. The interaction of these contradictory strivings results in symptom formation.

He then refers to the typical defense mechanisms of isolation, reaction-formation, undoing, and describes the attempt to corrupt the superego (as pointed out by Alexander) with the patient pretending to be obedient and willing to suffer, thus expiating the guilt before sinning, so that he can feel free to indulge.

If the patient succeeds in making analysis appear nonsensical, he utilizes the situation to prove that the analyst (superego) is in the wrong [a point also made by Freud]; then he can feel justified in his aggression; he may even succeed in feeling equal or superior to the analyst [see Ferenczi above]. Under these circumstances, he feels free to indulge in gratifications that were hitherto prohibited by his superego.

In treatment, the patient's unconscious equates thoughts and feelings with actions; thus, obsessive thoughts substitute for actions, and until the patient realizes that the two are not the same, he cannot indulge in thoughts or fantasies without consequent guilt and self-punishment. The latent meaning and origin of obsessive thoughts and compulsions must be recognized by the patient.

Michaels and Porter in their paper "Psychiatric and Social Implications of Contrasts Between Psychopathic Personality and Obsessive Compulsion Neurosis" (1949) remark on how little is written about "the factors which enhance good adjustment, or of the variations from the mean which may exist, without seriously disturbing an adequate adaptation to life and its many stresses." They try to substantiate the impression "that the compulsion neurosis represents a pathologic extreme of deviations from the mean which are generally useful in civilized society, while the psychopathic personality represents pathologic deviations in other directions which are likely to lead to difficulty in adjustment in modern culture."

The authors examined 1,383 psychiatric cases observed at Newton D. Baker General Hospital during 1944-1945 and were impressed by the distinct infrequency of compulsion neurosis (0.2%) among these cases, as well as, in the few cases which were observed, by the long period of service rendered (in the armed forces) before hospitalization. They turned to the literature for further clarification and found confirmation of its infrequency in military hospitals and as a cause of separation from military service. "In the reports of many large series of psychiatric cases, this condition was not even mentioned, although some authors (Rosenburg and Guttman; Wittkower and Spillane; Miller) called attention to the infrequency of 'psychasthenia' and compulsion neurosis in war time." The observations of the authors cited by Michaels and Porter refer not only to United States forces but to British and Canadian as well and cover both world wars.

The obsessive and compulsive symptoms in obsessionals are defense mechanisms which serve the purpose of allaying or binding anxiety. The authors point out that the army and navy "with their discipline, regimentation, reports, rules, regulations and their emphasis on orderliness, cleanliness and economy, may be considered as vast compulsive organizations" that favor the obsessional who finds the possibility of augmenting and strengthening his defenses while in military service. Those tending towards psychopathy on the contrary find themselves in collusion with a system (the army) that demands discipline and is restrictive.

Michaels and Porter refer to Grinker and Spiegel's book *Men Under Stress*. "Grinker and Spiegel found that men with compulsive characters often make good bomber pilots, since their rigid patterns of behaviour cause them to be steady and reliable." They also quote N. A. Levy, who, reporting on combat fliers, noted that "the excessively meticulous, perfectionistic, rigid, compulsive personality habitually defends himself against intense chronic anxieties by these ritualistic devices. These individuals on the whole manage to complete the tour of operational duty because of the compelling drive of their characteristically strict consciences and intense needs to maintain self-esteem."

Among other points, the authors' conclusions include:

The surmise is advanced that a degree of compulsiveness is generally essential to strength of character, and compulsive character traits are regarded as within the range of normal personality variants as distinguished from symptoms of compulsion neurosis which are pathologic exaggerations of such variants.

A certain degree of compulsiveness is considered worthwhile to all citizens of current civilized society as well as to members of military forces.

It is suggested that early training which instills some compulsive character traits in children by virtue of respect for authority remains necessary in our present-day culture.

Parker (1965), after briefly describing the treatment of two cases of obsessional neurosis, postulated that when a certain parental attitude named by him *marked authoritariansim* "is a strong factor in child rearing by an otherwise honest and loving father, elements arising in the parent-child relationship come into direct association with psychic residua of instinctual struggle at the anal stage, and made the parent-child interaction a focus for affect isolated at that time." He added that "affect aroused in the parent-child relationship specifically reinforces elements of anal conflict which are connected with the development of obsessional features, and specifically fosters the use of isolation as a defense mechanism" (p. 339).

Wilhelm Reich has made some valuable remarks as to the distinction between the manifestations of a character neurosis and symptom neuroses that will be referred to in a later section.

Rice (1974) uses an interesting case to describe some of his own ideas about obsessionals. Although he is clearly aware of the contradiction inherent in his view and discusses it briefly, his presentation suffers somewhat from the assumption that there is not enough psychic structure to think in terms of conflicts until the phallic-oedipal phase. This assumption, long a signifcant source of cenceptual confusion among psychoanalysts and psychiatrists whose experience with children is limited, I have attempted to clarify in my *Early Childhood Disturbances, The Infantile Neurosis and the Adulthood Disturbances* (1966).

Rice compares and relates phobias and obsessional neuroses to each other through a regressive process that leads from the former into the latter (this is seen quite frequently in children in my experience and will be referred to later on). He proposes the term *compulsive companion* as equivalent though obviously different dynamically from the phenomenon of the "phobic companion." The compulsive companion can be a parent, lover, spouse, friend or therapist. He says, "The object (meaning the compulsive companion), if he permits it, can eventually become a willing participant and prisoner, in bondage not only to his own needs but to those of the patient as well." Rice refers to it as neurotic variety of *folie à deux*. (In my experience this is rare with adult obsessionals but quite common in the case of children, as will be described later.)

Robinson (1974) discussed an obsessional patient with special emphasis on the role played by the patient's going to sleep during some sessions.

Rosenberg (1967), after examining the personality structure of forty-seven obsessionals, suggested that there was a close relationship between obsessional personality traits and the illness. Yet the results of psychological testing indicate a difference between traits and symptoms (p. 477).

Sachs published in 1947 an interesting paper, "The Transformation of Impulses into Obsessional Ritual," in which he compares the intensity with which the performance of the insignificant ritual imposes itself on the ego, (as well as the anxiety and displeasure ensuing if the ritual cannot be performed), to the situation when an instinctual wish is frustrated. The difference between these two situations lies in the fact that an instinct originates in the id, "whereas the obsession does not serve for the satisfaction of any recognizable id-tendencies." The ego in obsessional neurosis is subservient to another power.

Sachs differentiates between "obsessional rituals" and a "group of obsessional phenomena" (as described by Freud in the case of the Rat Man). Sachs writes that the latter usually precede the establishment of the rituals, sometimes by several years: "These impulses are mostly of an aggressive nature, very often homicidal or suicidal; they are cathected with great affect, rejected by the ego with the utmost energy, and followed by an attack of anxiety. The acts toward which these impulses urge are *never* actually carried out."

Further development of these impulses leads (1) to a form of anxiety neurosis (usually a phobia); or (2) to an obsessional ritual—the anxiety signal initiates repression of the impulse and, subsequently, in its place appears the obsessional ritual. Yet the impulse does not completely disappear, remaining as "mere thought-contents" without psychic energy or affect. Occasionally the impulse will erupt with the original, affective strength (viz. the Rat Man's experienced command to cut his throat and kill his beloved's grandmother).

There is a genuine instinctual origin for these impulses from the anal-sadistic level; however, slight replacements occur and the persons against whom the aggressive impulses are directed are not identical with the original objects. Sometimes the drive is reversed against the subject himself, in a suicidal impulse to which the obsessional neurotic does not give way.

A further differentiating point between these impulses and the subsequent ritual is the following: the anxiety bound up with impulses is caused by the urge to perform these aggressive acts, and yet this urge is never complied with. Conversely, the ritual, the compulsory demands, have no concomitant anxiety; anxiety only arises in connection with not performing the compulsive act.

Aggressive impulses to act belong to the id, and the anxiety reaction is due to fixation at the anal-sadistic stage or regression to it.

The anxiety signal makes for the repression of the dangerous drive; however, the repressed drive maintains its autonomy in the unconscious, the anal-sadistic fixation is reinforced and the superego's condemnation becomes even more forceful. Notwithstanding, the eventual obsessional ritual containing these impulses is free from anxiety.

This can only mean that the superego instead of punishing the impulses after they have succeeded in invading consciousness, now uses a more subtle technique of prevention. It insists that these silly acts, useless for all practical purposes, must be performed as a protection against the forbidden acts aimed at by the repressed impulses. . . . The rejection by the ego of the impulses, the refusal to act on them, the anxiety which follows this break-through, were only the conflict.

This implies that the ritual owes its origin and first development to the superego and not to the id. In the service of the superego the ritual supplements the repressed wishes, which are, from the standpoint of the superego, identical with acts, and forms an almost permanent "alibi."

The rituals are usually in relation to dressing, undressing, washing, excremental acts, touching, etc.—all typical occasions of infantile sexuality and auto-erotic practices. Sachs writes that "since the ritual is used finally, when it comes under the domination of the id, as a means of the return of the repressed impulses, it must originally owe its existence to the intention of keeping these same impulses in repression."

In summarizing, Sachs makes the following points:

1. Although the ritual is primarily a superego creation, id-elements, which eventually succeed in using it for instinctual gratification, are present from the start.
2. Usually the ritual is largely concerned with autoerotic tendencies.
3. The superego deals with aggressive tendencies above all reaction-formations, which are characteristically exaggerated in the obsessional neurosis.
4. Guilt feeling which persists with such reaction-formations indicates that aggressive impulses still exist in the unconscious.
5. Similarly, resultant anxiety if part of a ritual is not correctly performed indicates the still active unconscious urge for autoerotic gratification.

Salzman (1965) contends that phobias are intimately related to the obsessive-compulsive state and are operationally and dynamically similar to it. He thus questions Freud's position in regard to the relationship between phobias and hysteria. He makes the point too that a better distinction must be made between simple avoidance reactions and phobias, a problem that is compounded by the tendency to use the terms fear, phobia and anxiety as synonymous. Indeed, he thinks that some therapeutic failures are related to these issues. To him a phobia "is a ritualized avoidance reaction which attempts, like all rituals, to exert some control over nature through the agency of magic. The phobia is a ritual of 'no doing,' or inaction. The obsessive-compulsive syndrome, with its characteristic rituals of behaving or thinking, is likewise an attempt to control and influence the environment. It, however, is a ritual of doing."

He thinks too that the presence of phobias in obsessionals indicates the failure of the obsessional mechanisms. Thus he distinguishes four clinical forms:

1. Obsessional state without phobias
2. Obsessional state with mild phobic symptomatology
3. Obsessional state with moderate phobic symptomatology
4. Obsessional state with severe phobic symptomatology

Sandler and Hazari (1960) reviewed many of the definitions of obsession and compulsion as recorded in the literature and concluded that

the implication of all these definitions is that an *obsession* is an unwanted but repetitive thought which forces itself insistently into consciousness and recurs against the conscious desires of the person concerned. Such thoughts may include intrusive doubts, wishes, fears, impulses, prohibitions, warnings and commands. Neither reason nor logic can influence these pointless, repugnant, insistent and absurd thoughts, and they persist so tenaciously that they cannot be dispelled by conscious effort. On the whole they are recognized by their owners as largely irrelevant and irrational. A *compulsion,* in addition to having many qualities in common with obsessions, is generally thought of as expressed in action. It can be regarded as a morbid, intrusive, insistent and repetitive urge to perform some stereotyped act—apparently trifling and meaningless—which is contrary to the patient's ordinary conscious wishes or standards. Failure to perform the compulsive act usually results in anxiety, while once it has been carried out, there usually occurs some temporary subjective lessening of tension.

The authors further report a piece of research intended "to investigate certain character traits and neurotic symptoms which can be designated 'obsessional' or 'compulsive.'" They "have attempted to attack the problem of whether these can be conveniently classified in a way which is meaningful both psychologically and statistically." For this purpose a self-assessment inventory devised by Sandler was utilized. Their conclusion was that "the term 'obsessional' has at least two distinct connotations, embracing two relatively independent constellations, which we have referred to as the *reactive-narcissistic character* and the true *obsessional* picture. This latter constellation might possibly represent a continuum ranging from the *obsessional personality* on the one hand to *obsessional neurosis* or *obsessional state* on the other" (p. 113).

Sandler and Jaffee (1965), after discussing the question of drive vis-a-vis ego regression in neurotic disturbances, pointed out "that we see, in the obsessional neurosis, a disturbance which is the outcome not only of drive regression but also of functional regression of the ego. The latter shows itself in changes in the mode of ego functioning and in the evocation of specific defense mechanisms. The changes brought about by the functional regression of aspects of the ego may in turn secondarily interfere with other aspects of the ego" (p. 430).

They further postulated in the obsessional "a particular style of the perceptive and cognitive functions of the ego, a style which indicates a functional fixation of the ego at the anal phase" (p. 436).

Schilder (1940) has been concerned with organic signs he finds in some obsessionals. He considers that psychoanalytic literature does not sufficiently emphasize motor problems in relation to obsessions and compulsions. A number of obsessive and compulsive cases he has studied have shown "organic signs pointing to pathology with the same localization as that found in encephalitis. . . . These changes may be constitutional or they may be due to lesions in foetal life, to birth traumas or to toxic infectious processes of unknown origin" (see also Schilder, 1938.)

Sterba in his monograph *Introduction to the Psychoanalytic Theory of the Libido* (1947) specifically divides the anal phase of drive development as Abraham suggested into two subphases, the *first anal phase* (pleasure in expulsion) and the *second anal phase* (pleasure in retention). He says that the "second anal phase of the libido organization has great significance in the origin of obsessional neuroses" (p. 45).

Sifneos (1966) described a type of obsessional for whom intensive forms of short dynamic psychotherapy prove quite successful. The criterion he used to select them was the acute onset of the compulsive problem in an otherwise well-adjusted person, usually following an emotional crisis such as recent engagement, a sexual relationship, loss of an object, etc. Beyond this he looked at the general fluidity of the defenses, the existence of marked anxiety, a good motivation for help, good intelligence and a history of meaningful object-relationships.

Weissman has written an illuminating paper on the "Ego and Superego in Obsessional and Character Neurosis" (1954). He distinguishes between an "archaic superego" and a "genital superego," the latter being more developed, mature, and benign. "In the archaic superego the aggressive energy attached to the prohibiting introject is least neutralized and more closely approximates instinctual qualities. In the mature superego the aggressive energy attached to the internal parental objects is more neutralized and the object libido attached to the ego ideals is desexualized." He remarks that the mature superego produces positive feelings of self-approval, while well-being under the archaic superego seems merely to amount to absence of unpleasure.

He considers that "in pathological development, the archaically introjected objects are not predominantly replaced by the objects of the mature superego. It is such predominance of an archaic superego that may be of importance in the genesis of obsessional neurosis."

In normal development, the postoedipal superego is modifiable, and subsequent identifications have their effect. In pathological development, archaic identifications retain their original type of cathexis, i.e., unneutralized aggression, and function as a part of the mature superego. These early introjects have priority over more mature identifications, in governing phallic and pre-phallic (anal-sadistic) drives and in influencing the ego's mode of reaction to these instinctual representations. "It is this particular vicissitude of the archaic superego in relation to the latter developed superego which is considered characteristic of the obsessional neurotic."

He discusses the question of obsessional symptoms usually appearing first during latency. He quotes Hartmann, Kris and Loewenstein ("The Formation of the Psychic Structure"), who have said that this timing is due to the newly formed superego's being to rigid, while he attributes to the superego other factors which make for the appearance of obsessional symptoms in latency. If oedipal conflict is not successfully repressed and regression to the anal phase occurs in the presence of a less mature superego (predominantly magical and pseudomoralistic), then obsessional neurosis and obsessional character neurosis will ensue. In a chronic obsessional neurosis, the superego is permanently immature (archaic). If symptoms of a transient neurosis disappear, this implies that the superego has become more mature.

He points out further that obsessional neurosis is characterized by

1. *magical thinking,* which is the early operation of the ego according to the modified pleasure principle; and
2. *illusions of omnipotence,* which relate to introjection of omnipotent parental objects and is closely connected with the archaic superego.

He thinks that in formal development, object relationships at the time of the oedipal conflict replace preoedipal object relationships; these later object relationships, ultimately divested of their exclusively sexual and aggressive aims, become internalized as the mature superego.

He states that in obsessional pathology "the greater the capacity for ego maturation, the milder the obsessional pathology; *where ego regression is extensive,* the symptoms are more severe and merge with borderline and psychotic states."

In his paper "On Pregenital Compulsive Phenomena and the Repetition Compulsion" (1956), Weissman "questions the assumption that activities of play which discharge unpleasure during the pregenital period are necessarily under the sway of the repetition compulsion." He concludes that "investigation of early developmental phenomena of repetitive activity suggests a differentiation of normal repetitive play from pregenital compulsive behavior and compulsive symptoms." The last two mentioned are nonautonomous ego activities.

Wisdom (1964) describes obsessional neurosis under the following headings:

1. Obsessional actions and obsessional thoughts
2. Compulsive actions and compulsive thoughts
3. Compulsion to repeat
4. Ritualistic attitude

5. Hate and impaired capacity to love
6. Sadism
7. Masochism
8. Sharp ambivalence ⎫ which involve
9. Admonishing attitude ⎭ personal relations

He makes the following distinction between obsession and compulsion; *obsessional* should be used "for the aspect of an action or thought containing a wish, and *compulsive* for the aspect that aims at counteracting the obsession.... [However,] usually the manifest symptom is a combination or compromise-formation. Obsession and compulsion in this sense share the general characteristics of preoccupation and unavoidability. The essential difference in the common use of language is that compulsive stresses what cannot be avoided and obsessional stresses preoccupation" (p. 111).

Wulff in his paper "The Problem of Neurotic Manifestations in Children of Preoedipal Age" (1951) refers to specific forms of jealousy in obsessionals that are not limited or linked exclusively with genital sexuality, genital possession or rivalry with other objects. He thinks that early jealousy in the child (Wulff puts this at the end of the first year) is related to the early feeling of "belonging to me" and to anal cathexis, i.e., the desire to possess. He says:

In cases of severe obsessional neurosis, this form of jealousy can directly be observed in anal regression. These patients suffer severely from outbreaks of their jealousy, which does not always manifest itself in relation to a rival, but often lacks this clear genital-sexual character, and expresses itself rather in relation to close relatives, various acquaintances and even strangers, and even more frequently in the area of professional activities or unimportant interests of the individual. This form of jealousy is often connected with violent rage, sadistic oubreaks, the desire to chase the object away, to throw it away, to make it disappear or to destroy it. Precisely the same manifestations of sadistic rage can be observed in the young child, during the pre-oedipal phase, in connection with his jealousy.

The development of a feeling of self in relation to the object and of "belonging to me" which Wulff puts at between one and three years

results in a strong fear of losing the object and thus induces the ego to exert the greatest efforts in complying with the demands and prohibitions of the object, particularly those pertaining to training of cleanliness and orderliness and to conquering the archaic anal drives. In this process, the compulsive-neurotic mechanism of reversal is activated, thus creating the early infantile compulsion manifestations. We might possibly regard this "anal" jealousy, the strongly developed concept of "my" and the possessive feeling directed mainly to the mother, as the preciptiating cause for a premature ego development and for the ego's premature object choice, to which Freud . . . attributed the development of obsessional neurosis.

Wulff points to the similarity in the origin of perversions and of neuroses, while distinguishing between the sadomasochistic perversions and the obsessional neurosis. Both are characterized by compulsiveness; but in obsessional neurosis pathogenic experience

is imposed by an external authority to which the ego submits helplessly, weak by virtue of its strong anal cathexes. Later, after the passing of the oedipus complex, the external authority is represented by the severe superego, which replaces it. In both cases the ego shows itself weak vis-a-vis the constitutional anal-sadistic drives. The only difference lies in the fact that in the neurosis the purely anal component prevails, and in the perversion, the sadistic component. This, however, brings to light the second constitutional difference between neurosis and perversion. If, in accordance with Abraham, one subdivides the anal-sadistic phase into an anal-libidinal and an anal-sadistic, one may state that in obsessional neurosis, fixation and the subsequent regression pertain to the later anal-libidinal phase, and in perversion to the earlier anal-sadistic phase.

In 1964, at the Fall meeting of the American Psychoanalytic Association in New York, a panel was devoted to obsessional neurosis.

It was entitled "The Genetic Determinants of Obsessive-Compulsive Phenomena in Character Formation." The panel was chaired by Dr. A. Valenstein and reported by Dr. S. Gabe.

Several of the papers read at this panel were presented in the following year at the International Psychoanalytic Congress in Amsterdam, for which this panel was a sort of preparation. For this reason, only a few aspects of the discussion will be looked at here. Thus, Gabe (1965) reported Valenstein's introductory remarks as referring to the different ways the term *genetic determinants* is used, in biology and psychoanalysis, stating that "these points of view are not mutually exlusive. Biologists admit that there is no such thing as a purely genetic determinant of development, uninfluenced by environment, while the importance of constitutional factors was acknowledged in analysis from the very beginning" (p. 591).

Valenstein similarly remarked on the need to be distinctly guarded with respect to the possibility of major transformations of character. "To put it in extreme form, we would not expect an obsessive to end up as a hysteric. In fact, we do not expect an obsessive to change the essential styling of his character, but we do hope that with a successful analysis he will achieve resiliency that he did not possess previously and that he will no longer be rigidly bound by conflicts at an unconscious level" (p. 592).

Ramzy presented his paper "Factors and Features of an Early Compulsive Formation" (1966), which was read a year later at the Amsterdam congress. Essentially he postulated a discrepancy between concrete imagination and verbal facility that will add to the biological factor of the innate strength of the anal-sadistic drives a constitutional predisposition in the ego which would tend to favor the development of obsessionalism.

Valenstein reacted to the presentation by wondering if the spontaneous games of arranging, disarranging, and reinstating things in a repetitive fashion might not be forerunners of rituals, or some sort of proto-obsessional phenomena. He seemed inclined to consider such phenomena evidence of a constitutional predilection for the systematic patterning of behavior even before there is any question of unconscious conflict.

In the course of the discussion Myerson disagreed with Ramzy's proposition that compulsive phenomena might be due to a discrepancy between imagination and verbal capacity. Another discussant, Abraham Friedmann raised the issue of the possibility of a progression by increasing severity of obsessionalism through succeeding generations, citing the case of a patient who lived with his obsessional mother and grandmother. He noticed the severity of the disorder was most serious in his patient, then in the mother, and finally in the grandmother.

Ramzy in responding to various discussants underscored the significance of biological givens, recognizing that there are innate biological differences between individuals both in terms of the drives and in terms of the strength of the ego and its various functions.

David Freedman's paper, entitled "On the Genesis of Obsessive-Compulsive Phenomena," made a distinction between obsessivity as a reaction mode and obsessional formations such as those seen in obsessional neuroses, character, etc. He remarked on possible cases in which the neurosis is not the result of a regressive move but the product of a fixation in the anal phase.

Freedman took objection to the assumption that obsessional states are dependent on the strength of the aggressive instincts. He pointed out, too, the relative neglect of the role of early phases of development in the obsessional, excepting from his criticism Melanie Klein, Abraham, and Glover, all of whom stressed the oral contributions to the obsessive state. He too was impressed with the primacy of oral determinants in obsessional children, a point of view to which Anna Freud took explicit exception in her summary of the Amsterdam congress to be referred to later.

Paul Myerson presented his paper "The Genetic Determinants of Compulsive Manifestations," which was also presented at the Amsterdam congress. He commented that compulsive phenomena are related not only to the nature and intensity of the pregenital conflicts, but also to the absence of ameliorating circumstances or experiences in both the pregential, oedipal, and postoedipal periods.

Robert Seidenberg remarked on the absence in the formal presentations and discussion of references to the social milieu, as if obsessionals were the product of an exclusively internal process unrelated to reality. He wondered about such factors as the prevalent system of rewards, punishmentn etc. and their possible influences on the illness.

The following papers were all presented at the 1965 Amsterdam congress and later appeared in the *International Journal of Psycho-Analysis* (Volume 47, 1966) as the proceedings of that congress.

Bychowski (1966) discusses the fact that among borderline cases (or pseudoneurotic schizophrenia) a relatively large number display clinically obsessive-compulsive symptomatology "which under analysis may melt away and thus reveal the hidden psychotic core."

Greenson (1966) questions Ritvo's diagnosis in the case of Frankie, stating that his disturbance was more severe than had been assumed and referred to "the varieties of obsessional neuroses." Some obsessionals can be understood as essentially regressed hysterics. I think this is true of the Rat Man, as Freud and Zetzel have demonstrated. Other obsessional patients are people who have reached out for obsessional mechanisms as a means of escaping from some psychotic or borderline schizoid state of withdrawal. Did Frankie's obsessions indicate a step of progress from his childhood neurosis, or a regression? Or were his obsessional psychotic-like states perhaps a combination of both progression and regression?"

Grinberg (1966) discusses the nature and finality of some obsessional mechanisms (in particular, obsessional control), and the influence they have on the state of the self and object relationships He discusses two types of control. The one he refers to as the *omnipotent control*, of an obsessive nature, to be differentiated from more mature and integrated levels of the phenomenon, for which he proposes the term *adaptational control.* He believes that a failure of this latter type of control leads to the emergence of depersonalization symptoms.

Grunberger (1966) discusses the Rat Man with the intention of demonstrating that a deeper understanding of anality "would enable us to form a more coherent picture of the various aspects of obsessional neurosis." He tries to elicit "the common features of the various manifestations of anality and also to show that the anal fantasy always hides at some level a fantasy of more or less guilt-ridden anal introjection of the penis, as if anal encounter of a content and a container, that is, some archaic anal intercourse, were the prototype of all object relationships at this level. He calls attention to the importance and universality of the fantasies around the anal penis, which the patient must return but is compelled to hold back. Similarly, he rightly emphasizes the importance of the negative oedipal position and the strength of the passive homosexual longings, either a defense against the positive oedipus or frequently a regressive reinforcement of primary tendencies already existing in the personality.

Joseph (1966) in her paper points out through the analysis of a four-year-old child the economic factors that determined the emergence of an obsessional neurosis in the patient. She follows Melanie Klein in assuming that paranoid anxieties (from the paranoid position) when analyzed lead to an obsessional organization. She says: "In this way child analysis can demonstrate that the problem of 'choice neurosis' is really a question of 'defensive preference' going back to the earliest times of life. These preferred defenses can be used with varying rigidity against any anxiety constellation, giving a different clinical picture according to the underlying anxieties."

Kestenberg (1966) believes that "the observation of patterns of mobility and thought can contribute to the understanding of the sequence of developmental phases in general and to the genesis of obsessive organization in particular." In her paper she further states "that specific disturbances in the interaction between mother and child promote an anal form of integration that weakens phallic dominance, makes it vulnerable to stress, and enhances the formation of a rhythmic superego, characteristic of obsessive compulsive neurosis."

She also believes that on the basis of her clinical and developmental observations she can postulate the existence of two anal phases, "each characterized by its own dominant rhythm of tension and withdrawal-approach behavior." In contradistinction to traditional developmental theory her postulated *first anal phase,* described as the anal-erotic phase of sphincter-play, is placed between the ages of six to twelve months. The *second anal phase,* the phase of anal-sadism, is placed by her during the second year of life. She similarly assumes that there is an overlap between the oral-sadistic phase and the first anal phase and like others she emphasizes a certain genetic predisposition, so that babies "who in their total behavior evidence a strong preference for specific 'anal' rhythms are particularly vulnerable to maternal interference."

Morgenthaler (1966) remarks that the defense structure of obsessionals is on the whole discernible and stable. As treatment progresses there may appear a tendency to confusion which he believes to be an expression of an isolated ego regression. The latter affects almost only those ego functions that have built up the defensive organization.

Nacht (1966) in discussing Ritvo's paper remarks on the fact that Frankie's case (Ritvo's patient) "confirms the well-known clinical observation that obsessional neurosis follows more or less closely on phobic neurosis. The phobic defense gives way to an obsessional defense system. We hardly ever find, however, a case of phobic neurosis without some obsessional coloring, and still less do we find cases of obsessional neurosis without phobic elements, the link between them being, as we see, extremely close." Nacht referred also to the special problems of technique in handling obsessionals. One of these relates to the unconscious satisfaction from discussion with the analyst because of the erotization of the patient's thought processes. Another refers to the possibility of the latter's own defensive rituals being displaced by the analyst into the rigid and ritualistic application of technical rules. Nacht places particular emphasis on the need to keep an ideal affective distance between analyst and patient, but if this becomes too wide it would work to the detriment of the patient.

Further, he feels it necessary to avoid for as long as possible being drawn by the patient into the anal-sadistic material and interactions, since in his view this would help the patient avoid confronting the oedipal stage. In his view the obsessional "needs to have confidence, to love without feeling rejected, to be understood without being judged. For the obsessional patient this expectation is perhaps more cruelly tormenting than for others. The therapist must not disappoint it" (p. 138).

Ramzy (1966) called attention to the trend among clinicians to single out "for any event or any phenomenon one single cause, or only a few causes, to account for it." This in spite of our awareness of multiple causality. In this context he refers to Freud's statement concerning the multiple displacements from one obsessional thought to another typical of obsessionals. He tentatively propounds the hypothesis "that the compulsive person was a child endowed not only with strong concrete imagination, together with a high verbal capacity, but also had greater than average abilities." He concludes that "it is possible that at the root of compulsive formations is a combination of both an excessive degree of pregenital concerns and a strong inclination for the exercise of fantasy and imagination where concrete and verbal representations do not fit together; all of which occur at a time when the child has not as yet become capable of enough reality testing to enable him to put his pictures of himself and of the world around him in their proper dimensions and perspectives."

Ritvo (1966) referred to Anna Freud's comment regarding our need for a better understanding of the shift from the phobic neurosis with its bodily forms of expression to the obsessional neurosis with its predominantly mental symptoms. He stated that the existence of the report of the childhood analysis (the case of Frankie) "makes possible a correlation of the childhood with the adult neurosis" (p. 130).

He found that every conflict and symptom of the childhood phobic neurosis was represented in adulthood in the patient's psychic life, with the old phobic neurosis hidden beneath or within the obsessional neurosis. As he says: "The report correlates the predominant clincial form of the neurosis in each period, that is, the phallic neurosis of childhood with the obsessional neurosis of adulthood, and shows that the shift from one to the other was related to a normal developmental change in the child, a change that was facilitated and potentiated by the child analysis" (p. 131).

Rosen (1966) in his discussion of Morgenthaler's paper takes exception to his regarding the confusional state as a defense style or cognitive style rather than a "disintegration of defenses."

In his comments on Dr. Ritvo's paper, van der Leeuw (1966) remarks on the difficulties of analyzing the problem of rivalry with the father and the simultaneous passive longings of patients (as was the case with Frankie). He further refers to the relevance of masochism as a defense and to qualitative changes in the drives during analysis. Further, he explores the relationship between theory and technique during the development of psychoanalysis as a science, pointing out how theory influences clincial practice. He uses this background in referring to both Frankie and the Rat Man.

Wexler (1966) in his discussion of Bychowski's paper calls attention to the fact that Bychowski stresses the defensive character (rather than the restitutional character) of the obsessive-compulsive symptoms in the borderline type of patient. Wexler contrasts Bychowski's approach to that of Pious (1950). The latter emphasis is on the restitutional character of the obsessive compulsive symptom in the borderline, schizophrenic, or psychotic patient. Thus, he does not see it so much as an aspect of the defense activity, but rather of the restitutional process. Wexler makes the following important comment in this regard:

To say that the obsessive compulsive phenomena seen in schizophrenic patients, when it is designed to hold onto or resurrect object representation, and with it the sense of personal identity, is in the same defensive category as similar phenomena when they are designed to deflect aggressive or sexual drives, would be a considerable error. It would be like asserting that breathing is a defense against the dangers of oxygen deprivation, making thereby a useless and confusing extension of the notion of defense. Perplexity and obsessive thinking in schizophrenic patients go hand in hand. They stem from the repetitive effort to remember objects, object relationships and identity. The obsessive preoccupation of most schizophrenic patients with such questions as "who am I?" "what am I?" and "who are you?" are restitutional in character and come much closer to the fundamental psychic disaster which has occurred than the more neurotic preoccupations which defended against unacceptable drives and wishes.

Winnicott (1966) postulated in regard to the theory of obsessional neurosis the "concept of a split-off intellectual functioning which I believe to be an essential feature of a thorough-going obsessional neurosis case. The conflicts belonging to the personality have become localized into this split-off intellectual area. It is because of the fact of this split that there can never be any outcome in the obsessional neurotic's efforts and activities" (pp. 143-145).

Anna Freud undertook the incredible task of summarizing the views presented at the Amsterdam congress by the various contributors. That summary, in which she was assisted by Drs. Calder, Myerson, and Ritvo, is highly recommended and appears in the *International*

Journal of Psycho-Analysis (1966). Here we will present only her comments regarding her own view of the obsessional neuroses.

As to the range of obsessional neurosis, she says: "I have viewed it always as a specific kind of mental constellation, extending from the ego syntonic and near normal—during development in character formation—to the status of an extremely severe neurotic disturbance, bordering occasionally on the schizoid and schizophrenic proper."

As to the quality of the id contents involved in the conflict, she reasserted her conviction that these are the impulses of the pregenital (i.e., prephallic) anal-sadistic stage. She expressed reservations at the various attempts made to move the roots of the obsessional neurosis from the anal-sadistic stage into the oral phase. She thought that this was perhaps due to the failure of some "to distinguish adequately between the specific and the nonspecific. . . . Lack of a healthy earliest relationship to the mother has its consequences . . . leads to delayed or defective unfolding of many ego functions, damages the building up of a defense organization, of drive and anxiety control. But, and this seems to me a compelling argument, the resulting faulty personality development can serve equally well as a basis for any other neurotic or psychotic disorder or disturbance of adaptation."

As regards the defenses, "What I am familiar with are the following in various combinations: denial, repression, regression, thinking, doubting, indecision, intellectualization, rationalization—altogether a formidable array, all of them, with the exception of regression, operating strictly within the area of the thought processes."

She referred, too, to the variation in the symptomatology that seem to her "accounted for by the many elements which enter into its causation such as the prominence of either the sadistic or the anal tendencies in the id; the excessive use of any one or of several of the relevant defense mechanisms; the different rate of growth in id and ego; the prominence of either mother or father as the main target of the child's death wishes; the interaction between intersystemic and intrasystemic conflicts, etc. There are so many elements, and the possible combinations between them are so endless, that it needs not an analyst's but a mathematician's mind to calculate their number."

Chapter 3

Obsessional Neuroses
as a Facade

As you will have noticed in the earlier chapter reviewing the literature, there is a widespread notion that many borderline patients, or patients who turn out later to be psychotic, present intially with either phobic or obsessive compulsive neuroses. Opinions run in various directions. The obsessive neurosis phenomenon is seen by some as a defensive stance against a more severe underlying psychotic disorder—that is thus kept under control—at least in some patients. Other writers, thinking along similar lines, believe that there is a continuum between obsessional disorders and psychosis or borderline disturbances. They seem to represent two extremes of a continuum, that being the reason why some obsessional neurotics are said to transform themselves into psychotic patients. Personally, I believe that all the above is a misconception of what is really happening. This I will discuss shortly.

Further confusion gets introduced into our diagnostic thinking by the fact that the reationships between phobias, phobic symptoms, and obsessional neurosis are clearly understood by very few. Freud as you know considered phobias akin to hysterical phenomena, while more recent such authors as Salzman (1965) viewed them as closer to obsessional than hysterical phenomena. Certainly in the clinical descriptive sense there can be no question that some obsessional neurotics develop into borderline or psychotic patients. Others present with a variety of phobic symptoms. For this reason, Salzman, as we have seen earlier, described four types of obsessional neurosis: one without phobic symptoms and three with phobias ranging from mild to severe. To complicate matters further, it is not uncommon in the natural history of obsessional neurotics to find, on occasion, a phobic phase that preceded the establishment of the obsessional neurosis. In some such patients, the phobic manifestations disappear with the advent of the obsessional symptoms. In others, the phobic symptoms intermingle, side by side with the obsessional manifestations in various degrees of severity. In my own experience, a phobic phase preceding the obsessional developments is not at all uncommon in children. Some examples of this are given in another chapter. Frequently in children, with the advent of the obsessional neurosis the phobic symptoms disappear totally, as if the obsessional neurosis completely took the place of the phobias, ousting them—so to speak—from the clinical picture.

All these have led, I believe, to much confusion and to the various attempts at conceptualization described above. It is my impression that many such efforts have misfired and, rather than having clarified the issues, have further increased the conceptual obscurity.

The situation is by no means unique to the obsessional neurosis. A similar state of affairs applies to hysterical phenomena, though perhaps to a lesser degree. Nevertheless, the oral roots of hysteria are actively sought by many clinicians who feel dissatisfied with the anchorage of hysterical phenomena in the phallic-oedipal phase. Others have referred to the facade and/or defensive quality of some hysterias in terms of the more severe underlying forms of psychopatholgy. The latter range from severe depression to borderline schizophrenia or otherwise psychotic forms of psychopathology. A continuum between hysteria and psychotic disorders is explicit too in the literature, as witness the label "hysterical psychoses" frequently applied to some patients.

It is indeed true clinically that some "apparent or descriptively" obsessional or hysteric patients evolve in any of the many ways described above. I have used the term *apparent obsessionals or hysterics* intentionally, since by *apparent* I mean "in the clinical descriptive psychiatric sense." Yet, in my experience many such descriptive psychiatric diagnoses are essentially incorrect when considered from a metapsychological point of view. Strictly speaking, then, these patients are neither hysterics nor obsessionals though they present with such an apparent facade that descriptively their manifestations may well resemble closely the symptoms of such types.

We are all aware of the serious limitations of descriptive psychiatry for diagnostic purposes. As analysts, I believe we have better conceptual and diagnostic tools to deal with diagnosis and nosology than descriptive psychiatry can usefully offer. But we hardly ever seem to use them when dealing with diagnostic problems; instead we frequently revert to desriptive psychiatric diagnostic thinking with perhaps at best a sprinkling of ill-correlated dynamic formulations added here or there. Rarely indeed do I see a systematic approach to diagnosis, with our metapsychological tools used to penetrate behind the descriptive facade and to examine in minute detail the basic fabric and actual structure of the building behind the facade, before we affix to the patient the labels *obsessional or hysteric*. (The very problems discussed here led Anna Freud, Ernst Freud, Moses Laufer, this author, and many others to develop the "Metapsychological Profiles" for the assessment of children, adolescents, and adults. Indeed, it is the systematic application of such metapsychological diagnostic instruments for a period of fifteen years, first at the Hampstead Clinic and later at the University of Michigan, that has convinced me—and others—of the validity of the propositions I am trying to formulate here).

I will now try to clarify certain basic conceptual issues and to indicate the more common pitfalls in this regard.

First, there is the concept of neurosis, whether obsessional or hysterical. A neurosis is a very complex organization with a very specific fabric and internal structure. Clearly then, that basic fabric, that internal structure, consists among other things of very specific types of conflict, with certain instinctual impulses, against which very specific defense mechanisms are put forward by the ego. These conflicts belong to specific phases of development and have specific genetic determinants. They take place in the presence of ego and superego structures that have acquired during development and for various reasons very specific characteristics. Such conflicts, defenses and ego attitudes against them are closely correlated with specific fixation points acquired in the course of development and to regressive processes, the result of the stresses between internal forces and environmental circumstances of various types. Furthermore, we need the absolute certainty that the obsessional symptoms present are the result of the mechanisms of symptom formation typical for the disease and are based on this inner structure. Do not forget that we can see obsessional-like clinical pictures, in the mentally retarded for example. But, as I have discussed, the mechanisms involved are totally different. The presence of this inner fabric, this inner structure for any given neurosis, is as important, indeed more important than the presence in the overt clinical picture of symptoms that descriptively can be labeled as obsessions, ceremonials, or phobias. It is thus my contention that the presence of obsessional symptoms (in the descriptive sense) in the overt clinical picture of a patient, in the absence of the inner fabric, the characteristic inner structure of the neurosis, should preclude the diagnosis of obsessional neurosis, hysteria, etc. All of these elements must be precisely identified before we label a patient as an obsessional *neurotic*. Unfortunately, some diagnosticians will take the presence of isolated obsessional manifestations, or of obsessional symptoms in the overt clincial picture, as the absolute confirmation of the existence of an obsessional *neurosis*. They take some of the parts as if they were the whole. Furthermore, we are all well aware that isolated conflicts, remnants from the anal-sadistic stage for example, may lead to what are typical obsessional manifestations, or symptoms, following the typical mechanisms of obsessional symptom formation and conflict solution in a patient that has otherwise fundamentally and essentially an hysterical type of neurosis. We must keep in mind that a neurosis contains representatives, residual or otherwise, of all the conflicts experienced by the patient through the course of his or her development. Thus we can expect, in different proportion and degree of importance, manifestations in the clinical picture of various unsatisfactorily resolved conflicts from the oral, anal or phallic-oedipal phases. They naturally will have the stamp of their respective phases. All of them are represented in one manner or another in the final form acquired by the neurosis. Yet, the final form and type of the neurosis is an attempt at a synthetic integration of this multiplicity of conflicts into a single organization of enormous economic value. Its final structure (obsessional, hysterical, etc.) depends on the vicissitudes of the different phases of development; on the nature of the conflicts (including quantitative and qualitative considerations); on the main fixation points established as the result of the outcome of such conflicts and/or extreme frustrations or gratifications during the various phases; on certain innate and acquired ego characteristics; and on the nature of the superego finally developed—all of which interact with internally and environmentally favorable or unfavorable circumstances that will either advance development, create fixations, or promote regressive moves (see Nagera, 1966).

As will be expected, the results of such extreme complexity of variables in simultaneous interaction are very diverse. Yet certain factors, such as the intensity of the fixation point, will determine not only where the regressive processes lead but around which particular phase of development the ego has been forced to structure itself and organize its neurosis—an outcome that can only take place when it has acquired sufficient strength, usually around the phallic-oedipal stage.

With some patients the weight of the conflicts, the most significant fixation, etc. may be at a particular phase, such as the anal phase. Naturally, the ego will be forced to organize itself around that stage and those conflicts, but the result need not be an obsessional neurosis. It could similarly be a perversion, be that a homosexual development, an anal character, a sadistic perversion, etc.

For an obsessional neurosis to be the outcome, other factors will have to play a role. An example, beyond certain innate givens as to the strength of the anal component instincts, is the presence of a precocious, high-quality ego that objects to the anal impulses (and rejects perversion). Other such factors involve the type and nature of the superego.

In "ideal"conditions we will thus have a typical and *clean* obsessional neurosis: one that I do not believe will ever evolve into a psychosis and one that is not a defense against a deeper and more severe level of disturbance. Note that though there might be some residual manifestations from the oral phase, these do not shift the balance; since his fixation point remains basically that of the anal stage, this type of patient is not likely to take any further regressive steps into the oral phase.

If the main fixation point is the oral phase, we will, given other appropriate factors, have a disturbance and a personality organized at the oral stage. If the main fixation point is in the phallic-oedipal phase, we will have a typical hysterical development. The significance of these fixation points cannot be underestimated in terms of where the regressive move of the patient, given increasing stress, will finally end.

Unfortunately, not all cases are as clear-cut as the above. The developmental history of many patients is such that the fixation points are multiple (oral, anal, and phallic-oedipal) and the strength of such fixations about equally distributed. In this case we will have what is referred to clinically as a "mixed neurosis," with the symptomatic, behavioral, and fantasy-manifestations coming from all three levels.

Though the term *mixed neurosis* is used here, we have of course to be aware that in some of these cases the term may be inappropriate. These are cases where the multiple fixations, and perhaps more especially the oral ones, may have produced so much interference and damage, that further development from that point onward has been severely handicapped. The damage to the ego may be quite massive, leading to a "weak ego", its capacity to tolerate anxiety, frustrations, etc. being minimal. Its integrative and synthetic capacities as well as the capacity to deploy defenses effectively are similarly inadequate, and marked damage may have been inflicted too in its perceptual-cognitive capacities. Such cases, though capable, at least for some time and under favorable conditions, or functioning as a "mixed neurosis," are liable to break down under severe conflicts or marked environmental stresses. When this happens, we see a borderline or psychotic organization move to the fore. It is this type of patient that frequently presents like an "obsessional" before the final breakdown takes place.

Obviously too, there may be many obsessional manifestations as part of this "mixed neurosis." Yet this patient is not, strictly speaking, an obsessional neurotic. In fact such a patient, if stress increases, will abandon the phallic-oedipal position and will regressively move to the next earlier fixation point, the anal. In so doing, the obsessional manifestations, symptoms, and the mechanism of symptom formation will increase to such a degree, that at that point in the development of his illness, he will closely resemble (especially in the descriptive psychiatric sense) an obsessional neurotic. This may well lead clinicians who see him at this time to diagnose an obsessional neurosis. This is a serious mistake, since given the significance of the oral fixation the regressive pull to this phase is enormous. Under continuous significant stress the patient will undertake the regressive moves to the oral phase with a further deterioration of the personality, which may then show some borderline characteristics if the ego has been sufficiently damaged developmentally. Furthermore, in the absence of a strong ego organization a psychotic breakdown may take place.

It will be evident by now that I give great significance in this regard to fixation points. In the true obsessional neurosis the fixation is essentially in the anal phase, with little if any evidence of major fixations at the oral or phallic-oedipal levels. Expressed in quantitative terms, the anal-phase fixation is clearly dominant.

The relationship between phobias and obsessions deserves some consideration now. I have given examples earlier of children who initially presented with a clincal picture of multiple fears and phobias at ages ranging from five to eight. These phobias tended to appear at the time or shortly after the child moved into the phallic-oedipal phase. Such pictures, in some of them, remain quite active and florid for several years. Then, at some time during the late latency period, the phobias totally disappear and are supplanted by a typical and very florid obsessional neurosis with typical obsessive thoughts and rituals. We know too that another group of such children remains phobic no matter what stresses they are subjected to. In other words, they never regress toward the anal phase and the subsequent obsessional neurosis. A close scrutiny of these children consistently shows that those in the first group have an important, indeed massive anal fixation. This is not true of the second group, that is, those who remain phobic at all times.

I believe that what happens in the first group is that development proceeded to the phallic-oedipal stage in spite of the important anal fixation. As such they arrived at that phase too weakened to deal with its important conflicts. Typically, they became phobic as the result of their attempts to solve the phallic-oedipal conflicts. Typically too they used some of the mechanisms of symptom formation that corresponded to that phase, hence the florid phobic symptoms. Since the conflicts could not be resolved, the child remained phobic, at times for several years, until the stress was of such a nature that a regressive move took place to the main fixation point, the anal stage. At such point, the symptoms changed, as we would expect, into those of a typical obsessional neurosis. All these children had, beyond the anal fixation, the type of ego and superego that strongly objected to the now reinforced anal impulses and conflicts. The result thus was the development of an obsessional neurosis, for which they had, metapsychologically speaking, all the ingredients necessary. Those ingredients just got mixed together effectively at this particular point in their development.

This brings me to Salzman's point of the relationship of phobias to obsessions and his four types of obsessionals according to the role played by phobias in the clinical picture. In my view, when regression to the anal stage from the phallic-oedipal phase is massive, all phobic symptoms disappear. This is understandable, since the phallic-oedipal phase has been abandoned and with this abandonment the phobic mechanisms of symptom formation are no longer necessary and come to a stop.

When the regressive move from the phallic phase is not as massive, not complete, phobias remain present in association with the clincially evident obsessional symptoms resulting from the regression. The more cathexes that remain engaged at the level of the phallic-oedipal conflicts, the more florid and severe the phobic components present.

Though my line of reasoning satisfactorily explains the presence or absence of phobias with the obsessional symptoms, and even to some degree the severity of the phobias, this is not the whole answer. Phobias, as we know, are ubiquitous enough, but there are marked differences in terms of their content and "severity," as well as in terms of the ego reactions to them. Some borderline patients' phobias seem to have an ominous quality or "severity" to their actual contents. Similarly, their ego's reactions to them has on occasion a devastating quality. I have no definite answer to this problem though certain qualities in the ego structure seem related to it.

I should add that the type of phobia I am referring to here are those with clear symbolic meanings and dynamics. Other "phobias" such as those observed sometimes in the first year of life and the first part of the second year—for example phobias of vacuum cleaners—obey a different mechanism and lack symbolic value. The ego's immaturity has something to do with them and indeed the term *phobia* is probably inappropriate in reference to this type of phenomenon. This is perhaps another instance where they are descriptively similar and metapsychologically different.

Finally, I believe that a good metapsychological assessment of our patients should avoid much of the diagnostic and general conceptual confusion now predominant in the various areas discussed. By metapsychological assessment I mean going beyond the examination of the presenting symptoms and behavior. Typically, such an assessment requires dynamic, structural, genetic, economic, and adaptive approaches. This has been outlined by Anna Freud (1962), Moses Laufer (1965), myself (1963), and by Anna Freud, Ernst Freud, and myself (1965). Nevertheless, a few brief comments are in order. For example the impulses (component instincts) that are in conflict should be clearly identified as those corresponding to the anal stage, both libidinal and aggressive aspects (with the reinforcement brought about by the regression of those cathexes attached to the higher phallic-oedipal impulses). The presence of intensively active oral impulses and massive conflicts around them should alert the diagnostician to the fact that he may be in the presence of some form of "mixed" pathology and not really that of a typical obsessional development.

"True" obsessionals deal with their conflicts by use of the typical defense mechanisms described in an earlier chapter. Major departure from this type of defense organization should alert the diagnostician to the other possibilities. For example, excessive use of such maladaptive defenses as introjection and projection should be a warning signal that behind the "obsessional facade" there might be something of a different nature. The same is true when in the presence of obsessional symptoms with an absence of the typical mechanisms of isolation of content, isolation of affect, doing and undoing, displacement, reaction-formation, etc. The fixation point *characteristically* must be clearly predominant at the anal stage. Multiple important fixations, etc. should exclude the diagnosis of obsessional neurosis and alert the diagnostician to other forms of psychopathology and possible changes in the presenting symptomatology and its severity. The ego of the obsessional has special qualities of its own. The obsessional patient is usually well endowed in terms of intelligence; frequently there is a history of precocious ego development. The absence of such characteristics is an important warning signal. The superego of the obsessional is quite severe, and in some ways quite primitive and archaic, at least in regard to certain impulses (mostly the anal-sadistic ones). Yet some true obsessional patients show a superego that is very severe in some regards and quite permissive in others. The result may be a patient who is somewhat sociopathic in certain areas while quite intolerant and primitive in other areas of behavior.

The above is presented as only a bare minimum effort at a metapsychological assessment of this type of patient.

Chapter 4

Obsessional Characters and Obsessional Neuroses

The obsessional character is one of many possible outcomes in normal personality development and, where it remains within limits, a useful and desirable form of personality organization.

On the other hand, obsessional character formation can overstep these limits and come closer to the so-called character disturbances, character disorders or character neuroses of the obsessional type. Nunberg in his *Principles of Psycho-Analysis* (1955) defines individuals with a character neurosis as those "who are free of neurotic symptoms but who behave pathologically." Reich (1928) in distinguishing between character neuroses and symptom neuroses remarks that the subject only feels ill when the trait that has been built into the character becomes magnified. He says: "It is only when the characterological shyness rises to the pitch of pathological blushing or the obsessive orderlings to a compulsive ceremonial—that is, when the neurotic character undergoes exacerbation to the point of the development of symptoms—that its subject feels ill."

In the obsessional character disorder the limits compatible with normal ego functioning and normal object relationships have been transgressed, and the character traits belonging to the normal obsessional character are exaggerated to the point of becoming its caricature. Although the individual himself may experience no neurotic suffering or anxiety, other people will notice that there is something wrong with him and find him difficult to deal with. Such characters are hard taskmasters for others, while their own ego performance is usually affected to some degree. Also, their increased orderliness and meticulousness is disturbing to their environment, while they themselves take it as a matter of course.

Nevertheless, neither the obsessional character nor the obsessional character disorder should be confused with the obsessional neurosis proper, since the latter state implies a great deal of anxiety and suffering largely absent in the former. It is characteristic of the obsessional neurosis that it represents an actively ongoing conflict, in Freud's terms "an interminable struggle" between internal forces, while obsessional character formation represents a more or less successful attempt at solution of specific developmental conflicts which are brought to a halt by it.

Nunberg (1955) has pointed out that "character traits or habits are much better assimilated than symptoms, and form an integral part of the ego. The assimilation is frequently so complete that the distance between character and ego disappears. Then the character seems to be identical with the ego, which is never true of symptom and ego" (p. 318).

I have noted elsewhere (Nagera, 1960) the frequency with which certain neurotic conflicts or even neuroses proper are solved in childhood and adolescence by incorporating into the character structure certain traits and attitudes that avoid the ongoing conflicts. At the expense of accepting some limitations, inhibitions, and alterations in the ego organization, acute anxiety, neurotic conflicts, etc. are brought to a halt and a new solution is introduced that may be more or less permanent in nature. Nunberg (1955) has pointed out too that "the conflict between hetero- and homosexuality may be brought to an end either through neurotic symptoms or by character changes," as happens also with conflicts between erotic and destructive instincts (p. 319).

How far such a solution is permanent depends on numerous factors, among them its relative success. Sometimes the transformation of neurotic conflicts into character structures is only partial and perhaps therefore easily reversible. Many patients are known to oscillate between openly anxious and florid states of obsessional disturbance and more controlled ones without manifest anxiety, where it seems as if temporarily some of the well-known obsessional character traits had hardened up and replaced the more disturbing obsessions and compulsions.

---

*This Case Study was prepared by Susan Woods, presently a social worker on the staff of the Youth Services, Department of Psychiatry, University of Michigan.

Nunberg has made it clear that the "anal character traits" can be a continuation or repetition of instinctual drive gratification in an aim-inhibited or sublimated form (a child who retains feces may become an overpossessive and avaricious adult). Or these traits may be the result of reaction formations of the ego, with the anal instinct turned into its opposite (p. 305). A combination of both types in the same patient is not unusual.

What leads from these neurotic conflicts, or developmental conflicts, to character developments of an obsessional type seems to remain a two-way process. We have all observed well-established obsessional characters who have backtracked from the obsessional character to an obsessional neurosis at different speeds. Here the obsessional character oganization has crumbled because of renewed pressure on the economy of the personality structure, due sometimes to unexpected and traumatic experiences and life situations, excessive frustrations, etc. In some cases this occurs at the time of "change of life." Many others have pointed out this relationship between character and neurosis. Nunberg, to quote but one example, says, "there exists some kind of relationship between character and neurosis, particularly when we learn that a character trait may degenerate into a neurotic symptom. Normal and useful curiosity, for example, may deteriorate into obsessional questioning" (p. 315).

In the limited number of observations I have made of this reversal from an obsessional character to a florid obsessional neurosis, or to neurotic conflicts on the way to the development of a possible obsessional neurosis, it invariably happened that the "normal" obsessional character transformed itself in the first instance into a less normal one, i.e., into something more akin to a character disturbance of an obsessional type, and remained static as such for some time. Such a development points to the economic strengthening of the forces involved in the solution represented by the obsessional character. In this, all personality traits, reaction-formations, etc. become exaggerated, the individual becomes more obsessed with doubts and uncertainty, orderliness becomes excessive, and ego functioning can be brought to a complete halt. The degree of the changes that take place varies from one patient to another; it may happen that the process will develop no further but can be contained at this intermediary stage. A return to the more normal obsessional character oganization is sometimes possible as soon as the reasons responsible for the increase in the drive and defense activity disappear.

In other cases the above stage is just a station in the transit to the further development of a neurotic type of conflict or an obsessional neurosis proper. It is the neurotic suffering and anxiety suddenly present that mark the change from the character solution to the neurotic solution of the conflicts.

Chapter 5

Clinical Examples

The child cases that follow illustrate clearly all aspects of full-blown obsessional neuroses. They already show all the essential metapsychological characteristics of the illness later to be observed in the adult. This includes the typical defensive structure, the severity of the superego, the ambivalence, doubting, etc.

Yet, there are some subtle points of difference that deserve special attention. In children we see a highly dramatic and unstable clinical structure that is spreading quickly in various directions and involving more and more areas of the patient's life and behavior. Frequently, they give the impression of an acute situation in a fluid growing state. Case 1 that follows illustrates this point well, in addition to many others. Adults, in sharp contradistinction, tend to present with a more chronic and stable clinical picture. The impression is that of a rather rigid and well-established situation that tends not to show the continuous growth and marked oscillations more typical of the late latency child and early adolescent. Exceptions to this are the intermittent flare-ups of some adult obsessionals and the occasional acute type of form of presentation. By and large the disturbance is settled and has usually in the case of adults been well established for many years.

The contrast with adults is at times so marked that the child may convey the impression of a severe disturbance resembling, often closely, a psychotic type of process—a situation that poses special differential diagnosis problems. This impression is due at least in part to the fact that late latency children and early adolescents act out more openly their psychopathology and their neuroses. By contrast, adult obsessionals are more concerned that others will notice their obsessions, ceremonials, and peculiar behaviors. Through the years, they seem to go through a process of selection of the obsessions and ceremonials, settling down with those that are more easily hidden from the eyes of others, those that can be performed in private. Further, many obsessional neuroses in adults seem to balance themselves after many years in the form of "obsessional characters" rather than the florid obsessional symptoms that we nearly always observe in the child. These "obsessional characters" may on occasion decompensate to various degrees, at which times one observes more active and childlike obsessional symptoms. Indeed, with some obsessional characters there is little hope of therapeutic results if some degree of decompensation of this very stable character structure does not take place during treatment.

There is one other interesting difference between obsessional neuroses in children or adolescents and in adults. In my experience, children quite commonly involve other people in their rituals. They may demand the active participation of either parent in the performance of the compulsive acts or rituals. More frequently, as would be expected, the participation that the child wants to enlist—and is frequently successful in enlisting—is that of the mother. It is difficult for her not to give in to the child in this regard, since refusal to participate frequently makes the child panic or become, at the very least, extremely anxious. Further, since many such rituals take place around eating or sleeping time and such functions get seriously interfered with otherwise, many mothers have little alternative but to give in to the child's wishes. The same is true in the case of adolescents but to a much lesser degree. Case 3 illustrates this well, with the patient involving the parents in various ways but more particularly forcing the mother to "wash her hands" as the necessary complement to his own washing compulsion. He similarly involves her in obsessive questioning in areas where he has been forced to ruminate excessively.

The adult rarely, if ever, shows this type of behavior. As we see elsewhere in this book, he prefers to carry out his compulsive acts and rituals in private, usually feeling very uncomfortable and ashamed if he is observed.

CASE 1*

Circumstances of Referral and
Description of Symptoms

P.Q. is a boy from Ohio, thirteen years, nine months of age. He was admitted to Children's Psychiatric Hospital on an emergency basis on 28 March 1975. He had been noted by both parents to have had increasing emotional difficulties since the previous summer. These became worse during the week prior to his admission. His symptoms were primarily of an obsessive ritualistic nature involving repetitious behavior, compulsive repetitive hand washing, and gradual elaboration of rituals around bedtime. During the week before admission he was described as "immobilized to the point that he cannot get out of bed", spending the larger part of his waking hours in rituals, and being generally unable to function. His primary symptom on admission was that he found members of his family and certain objects "germy" and was therefore "unable to deal with them" His father believed the problem began in mild form during the previous summer, following a visit to his maternal grandmother. One incident during this visit involved a trip to a convalescent hospital, with P. subsequently being concerned and upset by sick or damaged people. He started then by being unable to wear certain clothing because "it was contaminated." As time went by, areas of the house became off-limits to him. Similarly, he felt that one of his stepbrothers "was unclean" (germy), a situation that soon extended to all the members of the family. They were all felt to be contaminated, with the exception of his father. His stepmother however felt that P. had been having difficulty for a substantially longer period of time. In fact, it seems that his symptoms had been apparent to some degree for several years, having started some months after his mother's death. The stepmother described the appearance of what proved to be a long series of "strange habits" about five years earlier during the summer. For instance, he began hopping every so many steps. That was followed by repetitive smelling of the table and the walls, eye-blinking, head-jerking and pausing with hands in

This Case Study was prepared by Susan Woods, presently a social worker on the staff of the Youth Services, Department of Psychiatry, University of Michigan.

praying position before entering rooms. Simultaneously, his peer relationships deteriorated and for a year or so now his brothers and stepbrothers had been teasing him about this behavior. More recently they had developed a strong hatred of him. Further, his symptoms had been increasing very noticeably for the five months previous to the referral to this institution. Thus, shortly before this happened, the Q.'s received a call from P.'s school one evening stating that P. had been trying to get through the door and out of his classroom for a period of over two hours. This Fall P. was referred for evaluation somewhere else, and therapy was recommended and begun on a weekly basis with a psychologist affiliated with the Department of Pediatrics of Ohio State University.

Three weeks prior to his admission here P. reported that he had "lost the key" to his mental processes. His parents were uncertain as to the meaning of this and could think of no precipitating events either within the family or with P.'s personal life.

Dr. and Mrs. Q. (P.'s stepmother) were eager for admission at Children's Psychiatric Hospital and it has subsequently become obvious that they are relieved by his absence and reluctant to have him rejoin the family unit. The Q.'s are involved in marital therapy at the present time in Ohio, the marriage having become very rocky as a result of the stresses of P.'s psychopathology.

P. expressed concern upon admission that there would be retarded or weird children at C.P.H. He was relieved after seeing the place because he saw no "weirdos" and found the hospital to look "very clean."

From the beginning P. has had a generally positive attitude toward admission, seeing it as "the only way to get rid of my problem." He can be expected at times to resent the family's splitting him off or scapegoating him as the one with the problems.

Description Of The Child

P. is a small, thin adolescent who has been described as an Oliver Twist type. Indeed he often walks around with a haunted expression, hair falling into his eyes, shirttail hanging out, holes in his pants, etc.

He hardly gives the impression of a compulsive personality, judging from his unkempt appearance. There have been occasions when he takes care as to how he looks. These times usually accompany a trip home or an outing with his family where he has enjoyed himself.

Upon admission most of his clothes were rather old and shabby. He explained that he had plenty of "cool" clothes but that they became germy after his trip to his grandmother's home. Finally P. was having to use safety pins to hold his pants together, wore no socks and had large holes in his sneakers (the only shoes he would wear). He was upset, crying when the staff finally felt that his father should be approached to ask him to buy P. some new clothes. Dr. Q. was angry and somewhat embarrassed, explaining that P. had many new articles of clothing including new shoes but to his and the family's endless frustration P. wouldn't wear them. Dr. Q. finally bought P. some trousers and socks and a new pair of sneakers. P. was amazed and overjoyed that his father had bothered to buy him clothes and had spent so much money on him.

Generally P.'s behavior in the various areas of the milieu were consistent. Upon arrival everyone was concerned about his need for repetition; for example, on his first morning at breakfast he felt a need to throw away and retrieve his milk carton numerous times, stating he had to "think right." Showers and bedtime preparation were another source of concern, often consuming the better part of the evening. Any attempt to interrupt the rituals or hurry P. were met by his whining and crying that people didn't understand him or his problem. A staff member commented that he had rarely seen such pain in another human being.

Group activities in the school and with his ward group also became problematic. Briarwood Mall (a large, new shopping center near the hospital) for example was germy because it was so "modern and weird." The arboretum later became off-limits because it bordered a cemetery. Most recently anything related to magic i.e., the color black, sparkles, glitters, psychodelic posters, record album covers, or book covers, movies about ghosts or witches, have produced enormous fear and given P. difficulties when trying to "think right."

Classroom behavior has been good and appropriate for the most part with occasional problems with some students. After Passover P.

developed an intense interest in Judaism, making a Star of David in Occupational Therapy and wearing it around his neck. For a time another class member drew swastikas on the blackboard. During T.B's vacation this rivalry became so intense that P. spent most of his class time in the hall voluntarily and began to carry a transitional object, a ceramic bunny, which he had made in Occupational Therapy. In P.'s Occupational Therapy group he is the oldest member the other children ranging from ages eight to ten. The group has changed from five to three members since P. was admitted. It is reported that P.'s intelligence, gross and fine motor skills and creativity all appear to be age appropriate or higher. Initially P. did not accomplish much. He spent much time perfecting his projects. The planning and organizational aspects of the project were difficult for P. For example, he wanted to make a Star of David and it was suggested to him to bend the wire to the desired angles. He rejected this suggestion and became involved in finding a mathematical formula to approach the problem. P. spent the remainder of the hour, approximately thirty minutes, attempting to devise a mathematical formula. He became anxious and frustrated with being unable to solve the problem. The next day however he was able to enter the shop and just bend the wire to the desired angle. This seems to be P.'s approach to problems—many times he must try to find a means of ordering or perfecting a project before he is able to work at a more appropriate pace.

Initially P. remained apart from the group. He appeared very anxious and withdrawn. He spoke only when addressed and interacted minimally with other group members. As he became more comfortable with the others he began to interact more. He appeared to be more at ease and seemed to enjoy the group. It appears that this group of younger children allows him to regress to behavior inappropriate for his age i.e., making animal noises etc.

P. approached his occupational therapist on several occasions, asking about her family and her practice of Judaism. These conversations were precipitated by her announcement to the group that she was taking several days off for Passover. Of late there have been no questions concerning Judaism.

P.'s concern about a family have been brought up on a number of occasions in the group. Once he made a family of ceramic rabbits and in a childlike manner stated "a family—isn't that cute?"

Generally P. relates well to ward staff and peers and is not considered a behavior problem.

P.'s relationship to two of his ward staff have been significant. K. and J. became vehicles for P.'s lingering phallic-oedipal conflicts, and were loved objects. P. frequently told K. that he wanted J. to tuck him in at night. He became anxious when he discovered his liking for J. was greater than that for K., and he found it difficult to understand that both could be loved in different ways at the same time.

After K. left, P.'s liking for J. as a maternal object developed into a "crush." He discussed her constantly in therapy, voicing his anger after learning she was married but seeing how futile his desires were because "she is a lot older than me." He wanted to be "mature" to win her attention.

During J.'s vacation P. decided that she was germy since she flew through the "Bermuda Triangle." Their relationship was over as far as P. was concerned. P. also knew that upon J.'s return she would become a primary staff and thus have relatively little to do with him. He attempted to leave her before she left him.

Family Background and Personal History

Mother: P.'s mother, H.Q., is deceased. A slim, dark-haired woman, she married P.'s father in 1952, and suffered a reactive depression upon leaving her mother. After the birth of each child except P. she suffered post-partum depressions. At each of these times Mrs. Q.'s mother would come to aid her daughter. Mrs. Q. felt her mother could "magically" help her to improve. Mrs. Q.'s mother was described in one report as an "aggressive unloving woman. Mrs. Q. seemed to thrive on her criticism."

Mrs. Q. was admitted to N.P.I. on four separate occasions for severe anxiety and depression. She was expecting P. during her fourth hospitalization. This is a part of the report of her psychiatrist:

> If I were to speculate on some of the psychodynamics, I feel that unconsciously Mrs. Q. felt she won the oedipal struggle against her mother. The patient's mother is a very hostile and aggressive woman who constantly yells and degrades the patient. Mrs. Q. felt that she

must have done something wrong and therefore felt guilty. We can see that since childhood and especially since the patient has been married any symbolic libidinal or aggressive energy (such as buying a house, having children, etc.) makes the patient very anxious and depressed as a reaction to her guilt and she seeks the reassurance and acceptance of her mother via the mother's hostile and degrading comments. The patient described a very hostile, symbiotic, sado-masochistic relationship that she had with her mother. She felt she always had to go to her mother who in turn would berate and belittle her, in order that Mrs. Q. should feel that she was still loved and accepted by her mother.

The patient went on to describe that she would even provoke situations as a a child which would cause her mother to yell at her and this would reassure the patient that her mother still "cared for her." Mrs. Q.'s mother exhibited both overtly hostile and passive aggressive attitudes toward the child and the only way that Mrs. Q. could retaliate was in her own passive-aggressive way by dawdling or doing things just the opposite from the way that her mother wished.

During her hospitalization Mrs. Q. expressed suicidal thoughts and fears of harming her children.

During her last pregnancy (P.) Mrs. Q. was told by her mother that she should never have any more children because she couldn't care for the ones she already had.

Mrs. Q. went to her father as a child for emotional support and felt he loved her more than he did his wife.

Mrs. Q. had a sister whom she viewed as "the bad daughter" and felt she had to be "the good daughter." Mrs. Q.'s sister has also been hospitalized for depression.

Mrs. Q. was always involved in aggressive battles throughout her life. In college she and her husband-to-be were in the same class. She was the valedictorian and he the salutatorian. She went on to obtain a master's in chemistry. On her third admission to the psychiatric ward she talked about her husband's attitude, stating he felt her hospitalization was not necessary and that she was taking the easy way out.

Mrs. Q. was tremendously conflicted about motherhood. She felt she was still a child and wanted to be a child. Mother's Day was apparently an enormous symbol for her. She was admitted once just before Mother's Day complaining that she "couldn't handle her life." On another admission she became "preoccupied", staring into space and complaining of being frightened after a conversation among the patients regarding Mother's Day.

On Mother's Day 1970 Mrs. Q. took an overdose of barbiturates and died two days later.

Father: R.Q. is a forty-five-year-old physician somewhere in the State of Ohio. He and his wife were both originally from Boston where they met and married while attending the university.

The couple moved several times early in the marriage, to Arizona, New Mexico, and finally to Detroit, where Dr. Q. completed his residency in medicine.

Dr. Q. was seen twice on Mrs. Q.'s first admission in 1960. He was quite anxious and seemed uncomfortable. He also seemed depressed and agitated, stating that he was unable to concentrate on his work. He intellectualized a great deal, saying that he thought his reaction was a typical one to a depressed wife. He added that he was quite lonely and did not like being away from his wife. He felt that if he could be with her he could be supportive of her as he had been in the past. Dr. Q. felt that the only person he could accept reassurance from was a doctor who was treating his wife. Dr. T. (wife's therapist) called Dr. Q. daily to support him and tell him of his wife's progress. Dr. Q. felt that this was not very effective in easing his anxiety but that it was all he had to hold onto. Dr. Q. also stated that when his wife was depressed he felt depressed too and when she felt better he felt better. The report of the treating psychiatrist goes as follows:

The highly interdependent nature of the relationship described above was confirmed by Dr. Q.'s statements to me that he thinks his own willingness to be constantly available to his wife tended to feed her dependency on him and that the two of them seemed locked together in the ups and downs of this depression.

One can assume that during this period there was little emotional energy for nurturing the young children in the home.

Dr. Q. placed a great deal of emphasis on the kind or quality of therapy his wife might be receiving. He was concerned that she be treated by a staff psychiatrist rather than a resident. He resented seeing a social worker about his adjustment to his wife's illness. Remnants of this are still visible in Dr. Q.'s wondering why neither he nor P. saw psychiatrists at C.P.H. He asked about his son's therapist's credentials. P. too shares these feelings, frequently asking what a social worker is, what M.S.W. stands for, and on one occasion commenting that he believed his therapist could probably help him as well as a senior psychiatrist. Dr. Q. is a rigid, obsessive-compulsive character himself. This became evident in his endless ramblings from subject to subject during the time of history taking. It was impossible for him to get through recounting a simple event without trying also to include every minute detail of his association to the event. He feels that his memory is poor and confused and he never ends satisfied that he has really told the story "right." He described himself as having a "stubborn streak."

Stepmother: This is the report of the parent's therapist: During the summer following P.'s mother's death, Dr. Q. arranged for a housekeeper, now Mrs. S.Q., to come into the home. She had just divorced her first husband and was supporting three sons from her first marriage. Her sons were away at camp during the first few weeks after she came to the job, and she recalls that P. was the first of the Q. boys to make friends with her. She had a great deal of time to devote to P. during these weeks and it was only when her own children returned that she and Dr. Q. began going together. P. then began to distance himself from her. When the marriage became imminent the following fall, P.'s siblings reacted quite angrily and P.'s more quiet reaction seemed to go unnoticed. Following the marriage P. became more and more withdrawn. He especially had difficulty accepting her youngest son, who is described as being quite different from P., i.e., rough and aggressive.

The family moved in 1971 to Toledo, where Dr. Q. practices. P.'s siblings were very unhappy about the move and again their more obvious behavior pushed P.'s into the background. One had problems in school and another became very depressed. O. cried frequently, withdrew, developed colitis. At his school's suggestion O. began psychiatric treatment of problems described as "similar to P.'s." This treatment has been ongoing to the present time. Mrs. Q. described the relationship between herself and O. at that time as very poor. O. is described as being much like his mother, the first Mrs. Q., bright and close to his dad. P. was closest to O. of all his sibs and would often try to emulate him (this relationship has now deteriorated to the point that the boys rarely speak). As relationships became more strained throughout this period it was more and more difficult for Dr. and Mrs. Q. to communicate with each other about the children. In 1971 the Q.'s daughter, B., was born. According to both parents her birth was greeted quite positively by the older children. Currently B. is the only sibling within the family with whom P. is willing to interact on his home passes and she is the only child who inquires when he is coming home.

Developmental history: P.'s mother was hospitalized at N.P.I. for the third and fourth time during her pregnancy with P., for symptoms of anxiety and depression. She was admitted and discharged in May of 1961 and readmitted in June of 1961. Just before Mother's Day in 1961 she phoned her psychiatrist and described suicidal thoughts. This pregnancy was obviously a strain for Mrs. Q. and increased her fears of inadequacy about motherhood.

P. was born two weeks early as was the pattern of all Mrs. Q.'s children. Labor lasted one hour and ten minutes. P. was a six-pound, eleven-ounce infant delivered under caudal anesthesia. Mrs. Q. recovered quickly with no complications for either mother or son. P. was breast-fed from birth and follow-up interviews with Mrs. Q. at N.P.I. found she experienced this as pleasant and took pride in the care of her infant. P. was described as a peaceful sleeper and he slept completely throughout the night very early on.

P. developed atopic dermatitis which Dr. Q. described as a red rash occurring in the creases of his body. He said that P. did not seem to be uncomfortable with this. For several weeks P. was put on a special diet in an attempt to determine the source of his allergy. Dr. Q. again recalls no difficulty or food refusal during this time and the special diet was finally stopped as the pediatrician seemed to feel it was not helping diagnostically.

Dr. Q. says that he recalls very few specifics regarding the P.'s age at the various early developmental milestones. However he feels that P. accomplished most things just a bit earlier than his two older brothers. For example, he believes his son held his head up quite early, was responsive to external stimuli and began picking up and playing with crib toys at a very early age. Although he cannot recall when P. was weaned it seems that it was fairly early and he does recall that by the age of one P. was feeding himself. While recounting this history Dr. Q. often interjected that he recalled his wife being troubled and anxious and on many occasions emotionally tied up within herself. He says that even though Mrs. Q. took good physical care of the children he feels now that they probably were emotionally neglected.

P. toilet trained himself at age two and half "almost overnight." Dr. Q. does not recall the development of P.'s speech but does remember that once he began talking he talked almost incessantly. P. rarely played with children his own age, preferring to spend his time with adults or playing with his older brothers. When P. went to kindergarten at age five, Dr. Q. recalls him telling long stories about what had happened at the end of the day. He also recalls himself and P.'s mother being amused at what a long story P. could make out of a very small event. The father remembers no difficulty in separation from Mrs. Q. when P. began kindergarten.

The following information was learned from the second Mrs. Q.: Mrs. Q. said that by the time she met P. at age seven almost all of his interests and interpersonal relationships centered on adults. He struck her as being a very dependent but cooperative child. She even described him as "a model child." She recalls that he always liked to have his things in order although he was not really fastidious. It was always quite difficult for him to get off to school in the mornings as it was quite a chore to get through all of his routines. By the age of twelve P.'s compulsive mannerisms and rituals had become a point of great contention between him and his siblings. Mrs. Q. remembers that approximately ten months prior to P.'s hospitalization his brothers began to noticeably withdraw from him and make fun of him. Before long all of the siblings seemed to be angry with P. It was also during this year, fall of 1973, that P.'s grandfather died. Although the parents would not characterize P.'s relationship with his grandfather as a close one, he did visit with the grandparents annually and seemed to greatly enjoy walking downtown with his retired grandfather and being a part of the interaction with all of his grandfather's "old cronies." When the grandfather died the maternal grandmother sent the grandfather's personal watch to O. rather than to P. Dr. Q. stated somewhat resentfully that this was typical of his former mother-in-law, that is, to be more interested in a tradition of giving a gift to the oldest grandchild rather than giving it to the one who had been closest to her husband.

The summer prior to this hospitalization all three of the older Q. boys were invited to visit the grandmother. True to form, only P. accepted the invitation and remained with the grandmother for about three weeks. Upon his return from this trip Mrs. Q. states that she began really pushing for help for P.

Possibly Significant Environmental Circumstances

Timing of the Referral: The timing of the referral seems to have coincided with the severe manifestation of the obsessive compulsive neurosis, however the problem in earlier more manageable stages seems to have been present for some time longer. Since P. often has difficulties determining when events happened and how long he has experienced difficulty, both the extent and duration of his symptoms are still unknown. He believes, however, in agreement with his father, that the major disturbance began last summer after a visit to his maternal grandmother in Connecticut.

This visit was an event for P. each year. He was the only grandchild who enjoyed these trips to Connecticut and last summer he went alone. This was P.'s first trip to his grandmother's after his grandfather had died of a heart attack a year before. P. had felt very close to his grandfather, more than to his grandmother whom he described as "mean and always telling me what to do." It is significant that P. was concerned to maintain the ties with his mother's parents. P. is also the only child who wants to practice Judaism, something which is frowned upon by the rest of the family but which was highly regarded by P.'s mother. It seems P. is trying very hard to keep his mother alive in a sense by holding onto the significant objects in her life.

Causation of the Disturbance: Four areas can be delineated as causally significant:

1. The mother's suicide. H.Q.'s suicide is a pivotal issue in P.'s psycho-pathology. He failed to mourn her loss, fearing that to express his feelings would be against his father's wishes. He is now engaged in the draining process of keeping her alive (which he believes his father, a physician, failed to do) by holding onto her traditions as previously mentioned. Significantly P.'s stepmother is neither Jewish nor religious and he resents the fact that the family has given up all Jewish traditions. A particular blow came on P.'s thirteenth birthday when his father offered him money and said that would take the place of being bar mitzvahed. P. felt this cheapened what is to him an important event symbolizing his "becoming a man."

In therapy P. had tremendous difficulty remembering his mother or any experiences they shared. He vividly remembered, however, the day she died and described it several times. The most significant aspects seem to have been when his mother was taken to the ambulance. She opened her eyes for a second and looked at P. He also remembered how angry his father became when P. told a neighbor that his mother was ill.

2. The father's remarriage. P. was initially warm and accepting of the present Mrs. Q. before she married his father. After the marriage their relationship deteriorated. She describes P. as acting like "a two-year-old."

The division between old family and new has continued to worsen. P. cannot accept his stepbrothers especially now that they "have changed." What this change entails is their move into adolescence with a concommitant increase in foul language, rough behavior and less care in personal hygiene.

3. The father-son relationship. In one session, P. described his relationship with his father as being like the song, "Little Boy Blue and the Man in the Moon," where a little boy all through his life asks for time with his father but the father is always too busy. Later the father retires and wants to be with his son but the son by that time has his own life and says he's too busy to see his father.

P. has tremendous difficulty expressing his feelings to his dad. He perceives him as all-knowing and all-powerful but very inaccessible. P. is visibly elated by the grief times he spends with his father but it seems he does not convey this when he is actually with his father. Dr. Q. describes P.'s behavior when they are together as passive, bored and angry toward sibs. When P. and his father are together they talk about science. P becomes anxious when he runs out of things to say to his dad. (This happens in therapy too.) He needs a mental script well planned out before he feels comfortable.

Dr. Q. is a rigid, authoritarian person who seems to have provided an atmosphere where P.'s feelings could not be exhibited. Childish emotions of glee or anger were scorned. To show them meant to risk rejection and withdrawal of love. P. learned from an early age to control himself, to measure up, to be adult in order to obtain parental acceptance.

4. Adolescence. P. wants to be a man but fears outdoing his dad. He has tried to avoid any competition with him so far. Now he is beginning to see that his father may have problems but at the same time he has decided that all doctors are perfect and able to overcome all difficulties.

Physically P. is small and underdeveloped. This concerns him because he wants to be strong so he can "beat people" in games and frequently talks of beating people up when they upset him.

He likes to be with younger children so he can be superior but resents their childish behavior.

Adolescence has also raised the unresolved oedipal issues which are central to P.'s difficulties.

Possibly Favorable Influences: P. is a bright, interesting, and interested child. He relates well to peers and staff and relates warmly to particular staff, mainly women. He is an attractive child and is frequently described as cute.

His interests are varied and socially he is quite sophisticated.

His parents though severely troubled themselves have engaged in marital counseling. It seems the family is trying hard to get back on its feet. What place P. will have upon reuniting with the family is hard to guess. P. has tremendous motivation in thearapy. He is insightful and frequently makes his own interpretations which are often accurate.

Assessments of Development

Drive Development

1. Libido

a. Phase development
P. is developmentally a preadolescent. He has broad interests in art, science, music, especially popular music, i.e., John Denver and the Beatles. He has good relationships with peers and adults but has difficulty when peers exhibit aggression which could be a physical threat, or when staff is authoritarian. He expresses dislike for the rules that are imposed and would like to live in the wilderness all alone, free from society's restrictions.

Oral Phase: The oral remnants are seen in P.'s occasional sucking motions and sounds at the end of therapy sessions, in his dislike of young children, and in the oral-sadistic rituals around food (putting food into his mouth and then taking it out, difficulty entering the dining room). He also has difficulty swallowing (he must think right) and he cannot eat, for example, at the Detroit Zoo because it is surrounded by cemeteries. (Notice the anal-sadistic connotations of this.)

Anal phase: P. strives to control his anal-sadistic impulses and fantasies with rituals and obsessive thoughts. One such fantasy he described as "the pool of imagination, a horrible, dirty, black gooey place that wants to pull me into it. Sometimes my eyes fall in." Whenever he thinks of this he must repeat what he has been doing to avoid anxiety. Unconsciously he is, as his stepmother described, "a two year old" expressing ambivalence, sado-masochism, tendencies toward stubbornness and rebelliousness. Reaction formation is P.'s main defense. The move toward adolescence has undoubtedly contributed heavily to this pattern.

Phallic-oedipal: P. describes himself as "curious George" and expresses an interest in sex. He developed a "crush" on one of his female child-care-workers but he found this relationship odd when in therapy he saw her as both girlfriend and mother and said "but you can't have sex with your mother."

Generally P. idealizes adults, particularly men but fears his own adulthood because it might lead him to be better than his dad.

P. is just beginning the adolescent phase and has not reached phase dominance. He is expressing an interest in sex though he is having difficulty with feelings of embarrassment. He has recently begun to discuss some of his sexual feelings in therapy. Often they have a decided oedipal component. Recently too he has shown some interest in a twelve-year-old girl in his class and behaved quite appropriately with her, as opposed to infantile behavior with another girl.

b. Libido distribution

i. Cathexis of self
Primary narcissism: P. does not have difficulty in primary narcissism. Secondary narcissism: P. considers himself to be intelligent with a good sense of humor, however physically his estimation of himself goes way down. He fears he is inadequate, not strong, uncoordinated and thus unable to successfully compete in athletics or engage in physical fighting with peers. To some degree his older brother's move into adolescence was threatening to P. and may be responsible for the symptom formation to some extent.

He believes he never got enough love or attention from his father. He desperately tries to prove himself to his dad but is always disappointed to learn how his dad "didn't notice" how happy he was to be with him. His chief complaint now is that his dad is strong and capable, so why shouldn't he let P. come home on weekends?

P. has developed a split between his natural mother as a good mother and his stepmother as the bad mother. He can no longer have needs satisfied by his real mother and he fears rejection by his stepmother.

P. is highly invested in his memories and fantasies of his mother. He recalls that when he was about four he and his mother had mumps. The whole family was concerned about them. P. became deaf in one ear because of his illness. He is identifying with his mother now and says he is a replica of her because he is hospitalized "for being crazy." He fequently talks of suicide when difficult material is raised in therapy. One day he even said that he tried to commit suicide by cutting his wrist with a comb but it only made white scratches. He said that he wasn't interested in really killing himself, he just wondered what other people would think if he did.

His goal now is to be like his father. He wants to be a doctor (a

neurologist) so he can learn how the brain works. He depends on his
father to supply him with the guidelines so he will not fail. His father
told him "a healthy body is a healthy mind," after his admission to
C.P.H. P. immediately began an exercising program. He runs
contests with himself. He wants to set records, which mean winning to
him, for instance brushing his teeth every night for a year. His favorite
hero is Einstein.

His relationships with other people are warm and accepting.
However, once a strong relationship develops and any hint of rejection
is present he rejects before he can be rejected. When he learned K.D.
was leaving, K. became "germy." When P.'s primary staff was taken
away from him and assigned to another child, she became germy. He
now realizes what this behavior means and says that if he likes someone
a lot they can't be germy for very long.

P. is dependent on external objects to regulate his self-esteem.
However he is capable of independent action and thought, the only
motivation seeming to be self-satisfaction. He has difficulty accepting
praise, usually laughing or saying "sure, sure," but it is obvious that he
likes it an agrees with it.

ii. Cathexis of objects

P. has the capacity to form and maintain relationships with peers
and adults. It often seems that the peers who become objects of
competition are rejected, for example, brothers, and a friend from Ann
Arbor whom he had not seen in several years. P. was excited about
seeing this friend again but this fifteen-year-old had matured and
grown quite a lot in the meantime. P. felt weak and small by
comparison and has not contacted his friend since. Very recently, he
has expressed interest in seeing him again.

P. attempts to control adults with his problems. "I can't do that
because of my problem" This has led to concern on staff's part as to
how much to push or give in to "the problem." At first P. would take
over an hour for an evening shower, and bedtime rituals were an agony
for all involved in his care.

P.'s closest and most enjoyable relationships have been with female
peers or staff. He was very proud when a young girl from fourth level
showed some interest in him (gave him a yo-yo and sat next to him at a
movie) but was somewhat embarrassed since she was "too young" for
him. His relationship with J. (female staff) has been primarily positive

but very much tied to oedipal conflicts. Recently he has shown some interest in a twelve-year-old girl in his class and feels she is "the right age for him" "not half as old or twice as old" as with his other two female interests. P.'s relationship with K.D. was good but he felt K. was not strong enough at first. Later he felt that K. was one of the few people who could "really understand me." Strong authoritarian men are seen as "fair" by P. though he resents their orders.

2. Aggression

The expression of aggressive impulses has been one of P.'s major areas of conflicts. Until quite recently he has denied angry feelings, particularly those addressed toward his father. However a great deal of aggressive energy is bound up in his rituals and obsessive thinking, which ward off his expressed fantasy of hitting people over the head with coke bottles (particularly vacationing staff) or sending authoritarian staff through a bologna slicer! For example, if he thinks of putting someone through a bologna slicer he must put them back through to make them all right again (thinking right).

Aggression is also seen in his tremendous need to control the environment. Angry crying spells and stubborn refusals often accompany change of plans for any unanticipated event.

P.'s aggression not only inflicts pain on the environment but is most often more painful to him. He feels tremendously anxious and guilty over his aggressive thought, and the rituals also serve as punishment for his self-perceived "badness."

Ego and Superego Development

a. Ego apparatus: his ego apparatuses are intact.
b. Ego functions:
Affected by and interfered with by his psychopathology, he is nevertheless clearly a highly intelligent child with reading skills, mathematical reasoning, and mathematical fundamental skills above his chronological age.
c. Ego reactions to danger situations:
P.'s fears are lodged in the external world in the form of fear of loss of objects. The id impulses are also feared characteristically because they may force him to become out of control and do things (show anger

or aggression) which would be severely punishable by his superego.

d. Defensive system:

Denial: P.'s obsessional substitutions utilize magic and rituals and are a defense which fosters power and strength in a world where he feels helpless and weak.

Rationalization: Since P. fears the "weakness" he thinks is implied in tender feelings, he recently denied his anger and sorrow at the vacation of an important P. C. W. by claiming she had a "right" to the vacation and he should not feel bad because it was her "right" to go away.

Intellectualization: Enormous energy is spent in holding back feelings by intellectualization. P. has such an explosive need to love and hate (punish) his father for rejecting him and/ or his mother but the only way he can deal with his father is through scientific discussion. He feels anxious if he is with his father without some specific intellectual topic to discuss. Unfortunately his father relates to P. in the same way.

Reaction-formation: Classic obsessive concerns for cleanliness, order, being good, are perceived as knowing the rules and following them, according to P.'s pattern. Paradoxically, he expresses a great longing to live in the wilderness free from human rules and regulations and living exactly the way he please.

P. also belches frequently and then immediately bows his head and whispers "excuse me please" sometimes three or four times in a row.

Doing and undoing: P. uses this defense in many areas but perhaps the most suggestive is his need to read a line and then "unread" it. For example, read backwards. This may indicate his need to know or his fear of knowing or the ramifications of the quest for knowledge, related to the suppression of information regarding his mother and her death. Extensive use of displacement, isolation of affect and content are noticeable.

e. Secondary interference of defense activity with ego achievements:

P.'s defensive system keeps him vulnerable to the fears he experiences in every new situation. It prevents him from learning by experience. He is so involved in creating reasons not to be somewhere or not to express feelings that he is virtually paralyzed by a system where there is no relief and where every day poses a threat of defeat.

f. Affective states and responses:

P. is capable of expressing a wide range of affective responses. He is a sensitive child and the potential loss of loved objects evokes anger, hate and guilt. It is only recently and only to certain staff members that P. is able to tell how he feels. Sad affects are usually masked by imitation crying or sarcasm.

P.'s self-esteem is low and this is particularly evident when gifts or praise are given to him. He says he never felt anyone gave him anything because they loved him but only because they wanted to "satisfy him." The only area where he acknowledges success and accepts praise is with his intelligence. Though P. is capable of affective responses and often displays them appropriately, his behavior becomes inappropriate when he is moved by a person important to him

P. is still somewhat egocentric and narcissistic. For example, he feels everyone thinks the way he does, and should, therefore, understand his problem. He is terrified of the anger of others especially if it might result in physical confrontation. Authoritarian people are disliked and criticized even when he believes their rules are fair and right. He whimpers and cries and impotently feigns rage when forced to do something he doesn't want to do. Often his responses can be described as overreaction. Usually the anger or hurt is not long-lasting though he tends to hold a grudge against those who have caused him to display negative affects.

Superego Development

a. Superego:

P.'s superego is overly developed, punitive, nonpleasure-giving, unrelenting, and constricting. The superego introjects which contribute to this pattern stem from the anal and phallic-oedipal stage based primarily on his overly restrictive father and his perhaps uninvolved, distant or permissively ambivalent mother. He felt he had to be good to win parental approval. "Bad behavior" meant risking parental rejection. The id has a need to discharge its persistent drive and the ego is left as the battleground for the two opposing sides. Normal childish feelings of gratitude, happiness, excited joy, sorrow, or pain and anger came to be viewed as weaknesses to be avoided, denied or isolated, so that he could be the good, calm, placid child he felt his parents desired.

b. Superego ideals:

The most obvious and most frequently mentioned superego ideal stems from his identification with the aggressor (father) and his wish to outdo or overcome his father. He wants to be a brain surgeon who will find the definitive cure for cancer and be the first to perform successfully brain and spinal-cord transplants. Not only will he be the first but he will be nationally famous and admired.

c. Other types of ideal formation:

Certainly his desire to become a physician is an appropriate ego ideal as his intelligence and latent personality strengths suggest. It is clear also that even as an ego ideal there is the apparent "identification with the aggressor" and his own self-desribed "little-boy-blue" phenomenon.

d. Development of the total personality:

In general P. has not reached age-appropriate development and may be found in the preadolescent stage. His over-all development suggests an initial ease in the developmental milestones without disruption.

There is no noted separation anxiety in Anna Freud sense of the word, and since he was the youngest child in the original family there was no conflict there. His illness, mumps, along with his mother at age four, served to increase his identification with her and left a permanent reminder of their shared experience.

P. did not want to attend nursery school (possibly a fear of separation). He recalls (or has been told) that he stubbornly refused to go and would not dress himself or allow himself to be dressed for the occasion. This is reminiscent of his present aggressive behavior around bedtime rituals. He states with pride "and I never did go to nursery school."

School itself was not a problem and both parents recall delight in observing P.'s reaction to it. We can only speculate that the kind of disturbance observed now, with its anal-sadistic qualities, indicates difficulties stemming from the anal phase, though toilet training wasn't a problem. The mother's frequent depressions may have contributed to these difficulties along with his father's authoritarianism. Mrs. Q.'s depressions continued to the phallic-oedipal stage and we may assume P. felt he could have given her more support and protection than his father did. The mother's suicide at the beginning of his latency caused an upset in this relatively peaceful period and sent P. back to using the defenses of an earlier developmental level and caused a hiatus in further growth.

Latency was accomplished, as seen in his adequate move from play to work, but the damage was there, P. recalls that his repetitions began at about eight or nine years of age, soon after mother's death and his father's remarriage. The suppression of information about his mother and the birth of another child served to reinforce P.'s feeling of being left out and unncessary.

The threatening arrival of adolescence was probably the last straw in P.'s ability to ward off the instinctual impulses and oedipal conflicts that were then reignited.

P. is now beginning to feel that he needs his father less than before and this can be seen as a sign of the impending move into adolescence. P. finds this very upsetting however, because of his paradoxical view of loving and hating his "all-powerful" father.

Assessment of Fixation Points and Regressions

There is a fixation to the anal-sadistic and phallic-oedipal stages, with defenses against regression to oral wishes and fantasies. This can be seen in his obsessive compulsive behavior and need to re-enact the oedipal situation. There are also some elements of regression to oral sadism as exemplified in his food rituals.

Assessment of Conflicts

P.'s conflicts have an internal and internalized nature. The internal conflicts are: (1) general ambivalence—his decision making is tortured, as when he wanted to give his stepmother a Mother's Day present but felt to do so might make her unhappy, even though he also thought it might make her happy; (2) masculinity vs. femininity; and (3) sadism vs. masochism.

The internalized conflicts reflect the internalization of previously external conflicts. There are regressive traces of the oral, anal and phallic-oedipal phases: (1) oral: eating difficulties previously mentioned; (2) anal: reflected in his fears of aggression, death, and his reference to death wishes, concerns with germs and magic; (3) phallic-oedipal: as seen in his crushes and wish to re-enact the oedipal triangle.

The latter is expressed in jealousy of his therapist and a female ward staff whenever separations are imminent or when they are observed by P. to be interacting with male staff. P. is also expressing some concern that his problems will make his therapist depressed, necessitating her treatment as an inpatient at N.P.I. There is an obvious sadistic wish here since he is angry about her impending vacation but there is also guilt perhaps reminiscent of the guilt he felt for not "making his mother happy" and thus preventing her depressions and subsequent suicide, for which he no doubt feels responsible.

Assessment of Some General Characteristics

Frustration tolerance: P.'s frustration tolerance is poor because of the pervasive nature of his obsessions and compulsions. He feels he must do his repetitions even though they take up a lot of time. If he is pushed beyond his own limit he will cry and become very stubborn and accuse people of not understanding him or his problem.

Attitude toward anxiety: P. is engaged in a constant struggle to avoid anxiety. The defenses he uses create the illusion of power and control and temporarily reduce anxiety.

At present, P.'s anxieties are so severe that he invests more and more time in warding them off. His obsessive rituals consume most of his time and overshadow all other events in his life. Despite their initial intensity they became worse during a period when P. began to ask questions about his mother and to criticize his father's handling of her death. After this the obsession took on a more magical representation (voodoo), attempting to hide the death wish he felt toward his father.

Sublimation potential: In view of the present behavior crisis it is difficult to judge the true sublimation potential. One can assume that it is quite high judging by his latency-age creativity. For example, P. is making a report on the state of Israel. This reflects his search for an identity and his questioning about his mother. However this has been interfered with and is now a problem for P. He may substitute the study of Saudi Arabia because he feels that too many magical events happened in the creation of the state of Israel, that the number *13* appears very often in its history. The one example he uses is that Israel was formed on 13 May 1948; Robert was born on the 13th of the month and his mother died on the 13th of the month.

Progressive vs. regressive tendencies: P. has a tremendous desire to move forward and be rid of his problem. He has the potential for progressive movement. He also acknowledges a disbelief that he will ever be without it or that certain areas of conflict will cease to concern him. There is also an element of fear of what would happen if he were no longer obsessive.

He wants to become an adolescent, mature, date, marry, go to medical school but all of these things pose the threat of failure or worse, success (outdoing father). Sometimes P. regresses, especially in O.T. groups when he is with younger children. Fear of a classmate and separation from a teacher several weeks ago prompted P.'s need for a transitional object, a small clay rabbit which he had made in O.T. was carried to school and brought to therapy.

Diagnosis

There are a combination of permanent regressions which cause extraordinary developmental strain, and crippling symptom formation according to the location of the fixation point and the amount of ego superego involvement. The symptomatic picture is that of an obsessive compulsive neurosis.

CASE 2*

This case examplifies well the very acute nature of the obsessional illness as it appears not infequently in later latency children and young adolescents. It further shows the lack of stability of the obsessional symptoms at the beginning of the illness. This is especially true of the obsessive thoughts and the ceremonials, that seem to spread rapidly in all directions as if the illness gets totally out of control. Indeed, the patients experience it exactly in that way; a situation that frequently makes them feel that they are going crazy. As mentioned earlier, this is in sharp contrast with the most stable situation of the adult obsessionals.

*I am grateful to Gerald Marsden, Ph.D., the therapist of the case, for his permission to use this material.

I should point out that in this case, as well as in several others I have observed, the very acute, wild manner in which the symptoms developed and extended themselves followed a sexual episode that seemed to stir up markedly the homosexual longings and conflicts of the late latency and young adolescent child. One gets the impression that the approaching onset of adolescence or its actual onset may play a role in this regard as well, perhaps by making the child very vulnerable to the homosexual content. Thus, this child's acute disorder followed an episode of mutual exposure of the genitals between him and an old friend of his. They both "took their pants down and looked at each other." Immediately afterwards he felt "awful" and thought that "God was shouting at me." He felt that this was the worst thing he has ever done in his life. He felt so guilty that he vowed at the time never to do it again, in fact have nothing to do with sex at all nor even think about it. The other boy in question was described by the parents (who did not know of this incident) as a rather effeminate boy who was ostracized by most of the other boys as being a sissy "who wanted to make me a queer." Though they have been friends for several years the relationship came to an end at this point.

R. is a twelve-year-old boy referred to our outpatient department by his family physician. The latter's assessment suggested obsessive compulsive traits but he thought there was an underlying schizophrenic tendency. As he saw it the main symptoms consisted of a washing compulsion of the hands as well as a need to take several baths each night. Further, when touched by other boys "he goes beserk."

On the evaluation it was found that the parents were first aware of a serious problem last summer where R. came to his mother "very upset," complaining of having constant bad thoughts though he would not explain what the bad thoughts were. The previous fall they had already noticed that R. was washing his hands and taking baths more frequently than was usual for him.

R. himself could remember some obsessional symptoms that were possibly two years old but that apparently he did not consider too disturbing. They involved such things as having to touch the door knob with the hand he had not used to open that door. Similarly, he used to have to do with the one side of his body what he had done with the other. For example, if he touched his ear with his left hand he was forced to touch his mother's ear with his right hand. Another ceremonial consisted of having to mention the names of relatives of boys walking with him, if the latter referred to anybody in his family, while walking through a certain yard, etc. He remembered too that when he was in the second grade (he must have been around seven) the teacher had shown a film strip having to do with germs. After this for a time most of the children washed up very assiduously before lunch at school, but he continued doing it long after most of the other children stopped.

At the time of the referral he was still forced to wash his hands very frequently and had to take several baths during the course of the day or the evening. The reason for this was that he felt "dirty." He appeared very upset at such times. At home they have learned not to interfere with these activities since he gets so distraught and anxious if anybody does so.

At the beginning, he had to wash only in relation to two boys in his classroom. He thought of them as rough and "bad." If one of them touched him he had to take a bath. Soon the thing spread so that he had also to take a bath if he touched certain things at school because they made him dirty. Thus, within a matter of weeks it was not only these two boys but some of the schoolrooms and the desks in these rooms that were contaminated, so that he had to bathe. Shortly afterwards it ·was all parts of the school that made him have to take a bath. This spread further so that just walking to school, touching any part of it or even looking at boys whom he thought to be dirty forced him to take a bath. Soon afterwards some areas of the house became contaminated too, as well as some members of the family, especially his older brother. While taking the bath he would avoid looking at his penis, sometimes covering it with a washrag. He never touched it, assuming that it would get clean just by being in the water. When urinating he could not look at his penis either though it was all right to hold it then "because he would wash his hands afterwards," which he always actually did.

Many other rituals were operative by now and constantly spreading so that he became more and more panicky and anxious. In order to go to school and back home he had to follow certain prescribed paths only. He had further to remember where he had stepped before, since the ritual forbade stepping twice in the same place. Naturally, he could not remember these places and as a result was thrown into a constant panic. At home too there were prescribed paths to move from one place to another with similar prohibitions about stepping twice in the same place, as well as places that had to be avoided altogether. Some of these pathways were to be used when he came home from school and before his bath, while others were to be used only after he had taken his bath and until nighttime. All this was naturally accompanied by much mental agony, confusion and doubting about whether he walked in the right path, in which condition of self-cleanliness, etc.

As to the baths, they too followed a prescribed ritual and of late he had to pay particular attention to washing his ears; he must open his eyes under water so as to wash them thoroughly. For the same reasons he had to draw water up into his nose and nasal passages forcing it down into his oral cavity and then out of his mouth!

During this time R. seemed quite angry with his father. He was also frequently abusive to other little boys both verbally and physically and frequently quite stubborn at home.

Further, while at school if he thought a "good thought" he had first to look at the palm of his hand and then wipe his hand on his pants leg. At home the same ritual was performed but only in regard to his "bad thoughts."

It is easy to imagine the amount of time R. had to devote to these rituals and the very crippling effects of all this on his behavior. His parents and siblings were both alarmed and puzzled by this most extraordinary behavior.

R. was started on intensive treatment at the hospital, where he improved very significantly after a relatively limited period of time. At that point he became quite resistant to continuing his treatment. Unfortunately his family did not see the need for it any longer since they thought by then he was back to normal again. Finally, they decided to interrupt the treatment in spite of his therapist's advice against it.

During the time of treatment there was never any question of his being psychotic or even borderline. It is my experience that this form of acute disorder at the age we have been referring to tends to respond quite rapidly to the appropriate interpretations when in the hands of a skillful therapist.

CASE 3*

History and Presenting Symptoms

At the time of referral for treatment R. was sixteen and one half years old. He was the middle child in a middle-class family residing in a university community in California. His father was a professor of music and his mother worked at the university library. R.'s brother, E., was two years his senior, and his sister, J., was five years younger than R.

The A.'s described R. as having been an easygoing, quiet child who presented few difficulties prior to the current problems. He got along well with peers and family members, and was a slightly above-average student since early elementary school But beginning at approximately age five, R. was beset by phobic fears consisting of frightening fantasies of burglars breaking into the family home. These worries gradually subsided over a four-year period but even into his early teens he occasionally would check the house locks carefully to be certain no one could force entry in the night. Apart from the intensity and duration of these night fears, R.'s development appeared unremarkable.

Three months prior to coming for psychiatric help, R. began to become preoccupied with concerns about lead poisoning. The A.'s home had leaded glass windows and R. started to worry about the possibility of minute particles of lead finding their way into the family's food. He had read earlier that lead poisoning could result in brain damage and the anxiety of his brain becoming damaged began to haunt him. He did not express similar concerns about other family members. In a bewildered and frustrated manner, the A.'s reported that no amount of reasonable assurance to R. about his safety from this perceived danger was able to quell his fears. Even "expert testimony" form a chemist friend was to no avail.

*I am grateful to Neil Kalter, Ph.D., who has kindly prepared and written the report of this case.

At first R. attempted to cope with his anxieties by developing a severe washing compulsion. He had to wash his hands for ten minutes at a time before each meal in order to remove any lead which he inadvertently might have gotten on them. He asked his mother, too, to wash her hands, though more briefly, before preparing meals. These efforts to manage his anxieties quickly mushroomed, and within a short time R. was spending over half an hour each time he washed his hands. Further, he had to wash his hands between four and eight times a day by then. (When I first saw R., his hands were red and raw-looking—he had taken to wearing gloves whenever in public to hide this condition.) As the rituals expanded he also began to appropriate knives, forks, spoons, and plates for his exclusive use. These were kept separate from the eating utensils used by the rest of the family. He washed "his" utensils for approximately ten minutes before and after each meal.

R. also began to insist that his mother give him verbal assurance that she had not touched a leaded window just prior to beginning her preparation of the meal at hand. When she tried gently to joke with him about his requests, he became anxious and even furious, loudly insisting that she tell him that she had not touched a window. Until Mrs. A. had stated several times that she had not been in contact with the leaded windows, R. made it impossible, through his incessant loud demands for assurance, for the family to peaceably eat together.

However, all these efforts to contain his anxiety proved inadequate. R. developed complex fantasies of how traces of lead could wind up in food. While preparing dinner, his mother might absentmindedly pet the family cat who had perhaps brushed up against a leaded window. Elements of lead would then be on her hands as she cooked dinner, thus contaminating the food. Or R. might have stepped on some small drops of leaded gasoline while crossing a street. He might track some of this into the house and his sister, J. might walk where he had. When she changed her shoes some traces of lead would get on her hands, and these would be deposited on the plates as she helped her mother bring food to the table. In a short time, R. developed many elaborated fantasies concerning the transportation of lead from some source or other, most noteably the leaded windows in his home, gasoline, and paints, to the kitchen table.

To counteract his increased sense of danger, R. began to insist on being given money to buy his own food. This he did, subsisting on large amounts of milk, peanut butter, candies, fruit juices, and dry cereals. The food was kept in his bedroom or on a separate shelf of the refrigerator which he insisted was to be "his shelf" and only food he bought was to be stored there. He drank the liquids directly from their containers and ate the food with his hands or disposable plastic spoons. All cooking and eating utensils came to be strictly avoided. But even with these precautions, R. could soon consume only part of a container of foodstuff, believing that the likelihood of its becoming contaminated increased sharply after being opened. There was no obvious weight loss evident.

At this time R. also began avoiding school, primarily because of his embarrassment over the need to wash his hands for such long periods of time. Instead he slept until late morning and spent part of each afternoon playing touch football with friends. Much of the rest of his days and nights (until ten or eleven o'clock) were spent in lengthy and numerous hand washings, and in shopping expeditions lasting nearly two hours. He went from supermarket to supermarket attempting to find food which was packaged in the safest-looking containers. To be safe, food needed ideally to be in glass or metal containers and vacuum-packed, although he often relaxed this rule when it came to particularly appealing items such as certain dry cereals, potato chips, and milk. He also continued to insist on assurances from his mother that she had not accidentally contaminated (with lead) any of the food containers on "his" refrigerator shelf by touching them. Professor and Mrs. A., seeing that R.'s symptoms were getting progressively worse, brought him for an evaluation some three months after the initial onset of his difficulties.

Treatment: The Early Phase

In the initial interviews, R. appeared anxious but spoke freely of his worries. He was clearly frightened of becoming brain-damaged which would result in his "getting dumber and dumber." He did not know why he had suddenly become so frightened about this possibility, and I had the impression that despite his belief in being so endangered, he knew in some small corner of his mind that his anxieties were not rational.

As keeping R. supplied with food, which he would only eat partially, was becoming increasingly expensive, I counseled the A.'s to continue to give R. a reasonable but limited sum of money weekly for food for the time being. This was instead of on the one hand not giving him any money or on the other leaving the amount available to him nearly open-ended. I also advised the A.'s to point out to R. that while he was having strong worries right now they expected him to be back in school shortly, especially since he now had a therapist to help him with these problems. At this point R.'s treatment began.

During the first several sessions the patient recounted the onset of his symptoms. His brother, E., had been home from his first year at college for the Christmas holidays. He had always looked up to E., a bright, energetic fellow, and was glad to see him again. They had roughhoused a lot as youngsters, with E. always winning. Still, R. liked to "wrestle around" with his brother, feeling close to him and liked by him when they did. While home for this vacation, E. came into R.'s bedroom and began to scuffle with him in their usual playful way. R. had been ill with a head cold and there was a thermometer on the night table. As they wrestled, E. pinned R. to the bed, sat on his head, and passed some gas. At that point the thermometer was somehow knocked off the table and broke on the floor. R. anxiously began to clean up the mercury and soon after started to worry about the possibility of getting mercury poisoning that would be followed by brain damage. Around that time there had been a story in the news, which R. had noted, about Japanese fishermen being poisoned by mercury from eating fish contaminated by unusually large amounts of mercury. Within a week of this incident his worries about lead began to emerge. His fears of mercury poisoning continued but were overshadowed by his attention to lead.

As time went by, I could talk with R. about the pleasurable, exciting feelings of closeness a fellow has when he wrestles with his older brother. And that when brothers are younger they are also curious about each other's genitals—that being one of the reasons they like to wrestle around, to explore each other's bodies. R. remembered how when they were about ten years younger E. would point to R.'s penis and laugh, calling it a "little thing," and would flick it with his finger. I pointed out that when they wrestled this past Christmas, E.'s sitting on his face after pinning him down must have meant that E.'s penis was close to R.'s face. I mused aloud about the similarity between a thermometer and an erect penis—both were hard, both could be inserted into an opening, a hole. R.. thoughtfully added that mercury could be like "sperm"; both were of approximately similar color and when the thermometer broke and the mercury came out it was "sort of like when you come." I added that when brothers wrestle they often can have sexy, exciting feelings, and ideas like wondering what it would be like to have their brother's penis rather than a thermometer in their mouth. R. looked uneasy and shrugged.

This discussion and initial interpretations of homosexual feelings toward his brother appeared to relieve some of R.'s anxieties about lead poisoning, a substance that could penetrate his body against his will and damage him. He began to eat dinner at home with his family about once a week, after these interpretations. He was also able to eat breakfast and lunch at home almost daily, at the kitchen table rather than in his bedroom. At that time too, about two months after therapy had begun, E. returned home from college for the summer.

R. had been delighted about seeing E., whom he idolized in many ways, but was simultaneously upset about having to sleep in his own bedroom again. Shortly after E. had returned to college, R. had slept in E.'s bedroom, avoiding his own room which he still feared might be contaminated by mercury. Worries about lead were still prominent and the patient made sure that his bed was repositioned far from the leaded window in hs bedroom. I spoke with him about his wish to be close to his brother, as evidenced by his wish to sleep in his brother's bed when he was away and his pleasure at E.'s homecoming. He admitted that he missed E. and wished E. paid more attention to him. I told R. that a part of him had learned that if he wanted to feel close to E. he could accomplish it by letting his older brother dominate him and by being passive to him. That had worked reasonably well in childhood but at his age letting another fellow manhandle him held new feelings and meanings, including exciting sexual ones.

Shortly afterward, R. brought a dream which had frightened him. He dreamed he was asleep in his bed and that it was very early in the morning. His door opened and E. came into his room holding a revolver. E. sat down on his bed and stuck the muzzle of the gun into

R.'s mouth. R. felt terrified and woke up. After his associations I decided to interpret his dream as a response to feeling terribly hurt and angry at E. for not wanting much to do with R. during the summer stay at home. He had wished E. would pay more attention to him even if it was a scary kind of attention. R. added that the gun seemed "phallic," and I pointed out that a part of him wished E. to stick his penis into his mouth and give him some "hot lead." R. laughed uncomfortably and said it sounded like a cowboy movie. I agreed and underscored the connection between lead and his homosexual feelings and current symptoms. Since he was appalled and frightened by these feelings he needed to find something else to worry about, that even though being frightened of lead poisoning and subsequent brain damage was terrible for him it apparently was not as awful as worrying about feminine feelings and longings inside himself.

The Second Stage of Treatment

Through the summer, some three months into treatment, R. became increasingly antagonistic toward, and frightened of his father. Professor A. was painting a bathroom in the house and R. was very worried about his father transporting lead to the kitchen, and ultimately into the food, via his contact with paint. Reality-oriented assurances offered by the family were no help to him. He became resistant to doing anything that would please his father and often went out of his way to be insolent. Professor A. was easily angered, and yelling, shoving matches ensued. R.'s anxieties reached near panic proportions during these encounters, as his father's touching him increased the possibility that traces of lead would get on R. or his clothes, and soon find their way into his mouth. My pointing out that he seemed to be partly responsible for bringing these episodes about and that this seemed to indicate that a part of him had a wish for them to occur made little impact on R. Similarly, interpretations linking lead and sexual feelings were lost in the roar of his turmoil.

There was now a five-week break in the treatment toward the end of the summer as the A.'s went on a family vacation to the grandparents' home, which was located in a resort area, and I, too, left for vacation. When we resumed, Professor and Mrs. A. reported that their trip had been a "disaster." R. continued to be terrified of lead, though he ate regularly and appropriately with the family, but was constantly provocative with his father. R. would make a gun with his fingers, point his hand at his father and move it close to his face, yelling, "It's a penis, how do you like that!" Professor A., frightened and at a loss what to do, tried to ignore his son as best he could. The A.'s frantically wondered about the possibility of hospitalization.

When I saw R. he related the same events that his parents had, but insisted that his father was provoking him. He spoke of his father taunting him about his fear of lead when they pulled into a gas station by saying, "Here it comes, here's that leaded gas coming right into the hole of the gas tank." The A.'s confirmed that the father, once enraged, did indeed lose his temper and "said things that weren't helpful."

I sympathized with R.'s plight on the trip. Riding in a crowded car for many hours without being able to get out when he felt worried was hard. I underlined his need to do battle with his father and that while his dad seemed to contribute to this when he became angry, we needed to focus on R.'s need to have these fights occur. It seemed to me, I told R., that this was very similar to his liking to wrestle with E. in order to feel close to him. Perhaps a part of him wanted very much to feel close to his dad in the same way.

R. then related how "passive" he had always been with his father. From the time he was six years old he could remember wanting to do things for his father and his father would take advantage of him. R. claimed his father would promise to pay him for helping with some work and would then renege. But "I just kept coming back for more." I told him that he must have loved his father very much to do that. He agreed and recalled with fondness the times his father took him to symphonies and recitals, explaining to his son the intricacies of musical composition. I said I thought he still loved his father very much, but that a long time ago he had thought the surest way to feel close to him was to be submissive. Now that he was a teen-ager being submissive toward a man had new meanings, new sexy meanings, exciting and highly conflictual at the same time. R. exclaimed, "But I'm sticking up for myself now, I don't do anything for him, I never give in!" I told him that the only times I saw guys have to fight so hard never to be helpful or pleasant with their dads was when they were very scared that a part of themselves did want to give in. Give in by being very submissive and having their dad treat them like a girl by sticking his penis in them. R.

claimed he didn't even want his dad to touch him. And I said, "But you
manage to arrange things so that he does." I pointed out that he knew
his father quite well and that he was also a clever fellow who knew
exactly which buttons to push in order to get a rise out of his dad. R.
grinned and gave several examples confirming that fact.

We continued to examine his battles with his father for the next three
months. I focused my interpretative work on his wishes to provoke his
father into a sexualized assault on him in order to gratify the part of
him that yearned to feel loved by his father. During this time R.'s
provocative behavior declined substantially. He added new dimensions to his homosexual conflict by recalling how his father had always
liked to touch him by putting his arm around him or playfully
squeezing his knee. He thought that was "queer" and that maybe his
father was a "faggot." I reminded R. that at one time he enjoyed this
attention, but that since becoming a teen-ager he had new sexy feelings
about being touched in these ways by his dad. The patient began to feel
more at ease with these developmentally cast interpretations and was
able to see more clearly the relationship between his fear of lead and his
worries about his own feminine, homosexual feelings. At this time,
seven months into his treatment, his fear of lead, while still present, did
not any longer interfere with his eating or his ability to sleep in his own
bedroom. He was also attending high school regularly and getting
along well with his father.

The Third Stage of Treatment

The patient now began to focus on his interest in girls, and generally,
on relationships with peers. The theme of masturbation as a
developmentally ubiquitous expression of sexual feelings was
introduced in the treatment, since it was clear that his feeling of
becoming a "dumb-dumb," or of being brain-damaged were directly
related to it too. He readily acknowledged his masturbatory behavior
and described his looking at magazines such as *Penthouse* and *Playboy*
while masturbating. In the course of exploring this area, R. confided
that he had been worried for some time about whether or not he was a
homosexual. He confessed how when looking at sexually arousing
pictures, he sometimes found himself "looking too much at the guy in

the picture." R. claimed he first noticed this concern when he was about fourteen years old, about the time he began masturbating to ejaculation. He went to his father and asked him if he was normal or not, and Professor A. assured him that all fellows his age had some ideas like that.

But his homosexual anxieties had nonetheless continued to worry him, albeit only to a mild degree, consciously. During one session R. described his recently looking at some *Playboy* magazines with another fellow in this friend's bedroom. I took this opportunity to tell R. that when a fellow gets excited by looking at pictures, and there is no one around except for another guy, these sexy feelings can get directed toward that other person. Though R. denied ever noticing that happening, the material in the sessions shifted. He became worried about Black men and Black teen-age fellows. Specifically, he was concerned that they would beat him up. Other men who "look tough," such as men dressed in laborer's clothes, gas-station men, construction men, etc., were also feared. I interpreted his fears as an unconscious wish to be "used" by these men, particularly in a homosexual way. He conceded that he imagined that Black men and rough-looking men probably had "huge cocks." I pointed out both his curiosity and his excitement, adding that that was exactly how young boys view their dads—with both curiosity and excitement about their big penises. R. was then able to recall the feelings he had as a little boy when seeing his father in the bathroom.

At this time, approximately ten months into the treatment, R. began to be worried about brushing his teeth. He also continued to worry about Black men and "rough-looking" men, but now his anxieties centered around the possibility of their having come into contact with lead compounds through the work he imagined they did. His fantasy was that he would get some lead particles on him and eventually they would get into his mouth (though not necessarily via food). Somebody who looked like a construction worker to him and who played in the touch-football games with R. would come into contact with him during the game. Traces of lead might then get on his clothes. R. might then rub his shirt sleeve across his face to mop off perspiration and these lead traces would be deposited on his lips. The next step would be for him to inadvertently lick his lips during a tense moment of the game. The lead would thereby get into his system with the ultimate threat of causing progressive brain damage. This refrain, in many elaborated versions, was repeated from about the tenth to the twelfth month of therapy.

Efforts to enlist R.'s healthy ego in the battle against his neurosis was largely futile. Attention to the fact that he was talking about such incredibly minute traces of lead only resulted in his pointing to the insidious, cumulative, and progressive nature of lead poisoning. Reminding him that his friends in similar circumstances didn't seem to be adversely affected brought forth explanations of the very slow, progressive nature of lead poisoning. Therefore, R. reasoned, one would not see clear-cut effects of lead poisoning until it was too late. Wondering with him why, of all the substances available, he chose to worry about lead puzzled him. Why not impurities in drinking water? Or carbon monoxide? This approach, instead of providing the groundwork for interpreting his selection of lead as a vehicle for his neurotic symptoms, served to open up new possibilities for the expression of his conflicts. For example, while these attempts to mobilize R.'s reasonable ego to look at the symbolic meanings of lead poisoning (given its unreality) had no observable impact on him at the time, some three months later he obligingly began to worry about breathing harmful amounts of carbon monoxide.

I soon abandoned this approach as unfruitful and instead pointed out to R. his fear of getting something from these men into his mouth. I reminded him of our earlier discovery about the connection between mercury, lead and his exciting, passive feminine feelings. It seemed that he was still worried about those feelings and that it was semen, not lead, that he was scared about getting into his mouth. During this period, R. recalled a time when he and his family visited his aunt and uncle and his cousin, S. R. was eleven or twelve at the time, and S. was two years older. One night the patient and his cousin slept out in the backyard in a small camping tent. S. showed him his penis, and also rubbed R.'s penis. He remembered being frightened and thinking, "What is he doing?" I empathized with how scared he must have been, but also how curious and excited most fellows would be in that situation. R. angrily railed against his "faggot" and "queer" cousin, and asked if that could be one of the reasons he had his current problems. I told him it was possible because he might have begun wondering whether he was queer after that. Especially since he probably felt guilty about the fact that a part of him quite likely experienced what had happened as pleasurably exciting. He accepted this but denied any occurrence of fellatio between himself and S. Nor could he recollect any curiosity or impulse concerning fellatio.

I continued to interpret R.'s fears about brushing his teeth and of getting lead poisoning via contact with certain men as representations of his homsexual wishes and the conflict he experienced around these forbidden impulses. I especially emphasized the internalized nature of his neurotic symptoms, pointing out the extreme measures he felt he must take in order to avoid recognizing that a part of him did have the feminine longings he so strongly objected to. His symptoms, as uncomfortable and limiting as they could be, were preferred to the realization that a part of him had feminine sexual wishes. Relying on his earlier favorable reaction to placing his difficulties in a developmental perspective, I asked him what he found so unusual about boys having a feminine part to their personality. They were raised by their mother as well as their father; wasn't it reasonable to assume that in growing up boys would take on some (feminine) aspects of their mother? Again R. found this both supportive and understandable. It seemed that his support, in conjunction with the interpretive work around his homosexual wishes, was responsible for the cessation of his fears of lead, of brushing his teeth, and of Black men and rough-looking men. This was approximately in the fourteenth month of treatment.

The school year was about to end. Suddenly, fears of becoming brain-damaged through carbon-monoxide poisoning emerged. He had fantasies of getting too close to old cars just as they were started, and of inhaling large amounts of carbon monoxide from the cloud of exhaust. He became fearful of walking to and from his therapy sessions because of the number of streets he had to cross and the exposure to carbon-monoxide fumes from the traffic. Occasionally, he could not remember exactly how close he had been standing to a car as it started. Retrospectively, it seemed to him he was only a foot away, but he also remembered being at least a half block distant. Several times he thought, on recalling an incident, that he might even have had the exhaust pipe in his mouth. This thought terrified R. Yet he knew he really had not done that. In this, unlike with his earlier symptoms, there was a major ego-alien aspect to his fantasies. I interpreted again his homosexual longings, emphasizing that he was the producer and director of his fantasies, and had "written the script" about himself sucking the exhaust pipe. He ruefully commented that it sure seemed homosexual. I agreed with him, and showed R. that this was like his fears of mercury and lead in that he was frightened of something dangerous and scary getting in his mouth, something that would change him. I wondered out loud if perhaps the idea of his losing his intelligence, his intellectual abilities through brain damage, might represent an even more terrible loss, namely losing his penis. He looked surprised and told me about his damaged "gross" finger. Apparently, he had had a crush on a girl named J. when he was fourteen. His family and her's were friendly, and one day he and his parents visited J. and her parents at their summer home, a car ride of about two hours. R. and J. were exploring a large, old house and came to a trapdoor leading to the attic. He climbed a ladder to the trapdoor and lifted it. The door slipped and R.'s middle finger was caught in the door. The tip of the finger was partially severed, just barely connected to the rest of the finger. His father and J.'s father drove him to a nearby hospital where his finger was stitched. However, it remained misshapen at the top. He recalled how frightened he was because "there was a lot of blood and I thought they's have to amputate it." I said I thought that was a hell of a thing to have happen, especially when a fellow is alone with a girl he has a crush on. In fact, a part of his mind may have concluded that sexy feelings toward girls were dangerous because when you have them something could get cut off. I wondered if maybe he equated his finger with his penis. R. slowly said, "Well, it is the fucking finger" (for the finger gesture). He went on to say that he supposed the trapdoor was like a "pussy." He had heard stories of girls getting angry at a fellow and during intercourse closing their legs quickly and twisting off the man's penis. I speculated to R. that his accident made that story, which many guys tell to one another at his age, have a special frightening impact on him. Perhaps enough to get him very worried when he began to have the usual sexy feeling toward girls that all fellows have. During this summer R. had difficulty getting himself to look for a part-time job. He very much wanted one, but he imagined he would become frightened of lead or carbon monoxide again if he had to work in a place which had chipped paint or poor ventilation, or which was around gasoline (e.g., mowing lawns with a power mower), and so forth. I reminded him of the various meanings of these fears and added when he felt feminine it seemed to mean not only having a man assault him sexually, but also that he would be *just like* a girl, namely that he would lose his penis. I again interpreted the connection between becoming brain-damaged and losing his penis, and who did not have a penis?—girls, of course. Within a week he applied for and obtained a part-time janitorial job for the remainder of the summer.

The Fourth Stage of the Treatment

After my three-week vacation we resumed treatment. By this time it had been seventeen months since R. had started treatment. Fears of mercury, lead, and carbon monoxide, and the behaviors they had been connected with (i.e., eating, sports activities with Black men and particularly masculine-looking men, house painting, walking near heavily trafficked streets, etc.) were alluded to in terms of "how things used to be." Occasionally, he became concerned that these different worries and obsessive thoughts would be re-evoked. But for the most part, this was a quiescent period.

R. now talked more about his interest in girls and his feelings of social awkwardness when with a group which included girls. He imagined they would think he was "dumb." I pointed out the interesting connection between this idea and his fantasy of becoming brain-damaged. Since we knew the latter was a representation of the worry about losing his penis, perhaps the notion of being successul with girls made him frightened of losing his penis. Interpretations of this sort seemed to have little effect on him. He continued to bemoan his lack of ability to feel comfortable with girls. He constantly felt nervous and awkward. And yet he seemed in part to relish this situation. He began many sessions with a self-conscious laugh which served as an introduction to still another episode involving girls in which he had felt awkward, dumb, and at a loss for words. I confronted him with this observation, adding that if he could convince both of us of his hopeless inadequacy then he didn't have to face the apparently terrifying possibility of having some girl like him and perhaps go out on a date with her. R. seemed stunned by this and later asked, "You mean I'm making myself believe I'm a jerk so that I won't have to maybe fuck a girl?"

Through this period of treatment he was getting ready for graduation from high school. He had had to continue for an additional semester and be graduated in January rather than in the previous June, since he had received several "incompletes" in courses at the time that his symptoms made going to school difficult. He very much wanted to graduate and go on to college, but his neurotic conflicts were starting to interfere with this. Thus, he continued to cut one particular class, which, if failed, would result in his not graduating. I was able to show him that although we both knew how much he wanted to graduate and go on to college, there was a part of him working to sabotage his attempt to realize his goal.

I reminded him of a comment he had made several times early in the treatment that "my dad and I aways argue lately and it seems that there always has to be a winner—it's usually him." I told him that graduation from high school marked an important point in a young man's life; it was a masculine accomplishment. I wondered aloud if perhaps a part of him felt that his father would not like this. Perhaps he was attempting to avoid being an assertive young man in order to remain "daddy's little boy" instead of becoming his father's competitor. Shortly thereafter, R. began to fear the x-rays he received at the dentist's office as part of his routine yearly visit. He imagined these would make him sterile or perhaps result in brain damage. At the same time he had a series of "accidents" in which he would bump his head on various objects, such as a chandelier in a friend's house, and soon he began to worry that these blows might have resulted in some brain injury.

Through this time he steadfastly refused to visit a physician to be examined for these apparently minor head injuries. But he worried about them constantly. I interpreted his need to punish himself in two ways: first by imagining something awful happening to him (brain damage), and second by perpetuating his state of anxiety and uncertainty about the possible effects of his head injuries by not seeking out a physician. It seemed to me, I mused, that he must be feeling terribly guilty about something. I wondered with him if this could be due to his competitive feelings toward his father around the issue of his upcoming graduation. Here his masculinity was embodied in his head, in his intellectual abilities and that was just what he was frightened about losing. R. added, "You mean I'm really worried about losing my cock?" I agreed, pointing out that his fear of x-rays centered around both his head and his genitals (brain damage and sterility). This seemed to help R., as he was able to graduate and then apply for admission to a nearby university. He was accepted for the winter term and began attending classes in January.

His conflicts over academic success were still much in evidence as he began college. He did not do the homework assignments which counted toward his final grade in two courses, delayed obtaining course-required books in two other courses, and turned in term papers late, the latter when he clearly knew that he would be penalized a grade for doing so (e.g., even if the papers deserved an A, he would receive a B). During this semester I continued to point out his neurotic need to undermine his efforts in order to protect his father from his competitive and hostile impulses.

It was while attending this first semester of college that R. began to fear he had Kleinfelter's Syndrome. His hips appeared to him to be overly large and femininely soft-looking, and his shoulders too narrow. He had not yet begun to shave, and he took this as further evidence of this disease. I interpreted his new fear as an expression of his feminine wishes; he seemed to be worried about turning into a girl. I linked this to his need to retreat from feeling assertive and masculine. He was a "college man" and apparently he found that very frightening. We continued to focus on his castration anxiety and his retreat to feminine concerns as a defense against it. I reminded him of how he told me he felt as a young boy—that he always had to give in to his dad and be submissive, and that a part of him was trying to do that again by feeling passive and feminine.

His concerns about having Kleinfelter's Syndrome soon subsided, but he complained of feeling "depressed about girls." He would never have a girlfriend, he was too thin, too young-looking, as he did not shave and had no beard. I confronted his feelings of hopelessness and told him that that was exactly how a boy of four or five feels when he wishes his mother would prefer him to his father. A boy's father seems so big, so strong, so accomplished that the thought of wresting mother's affections from him indeed seems hopeless. Rather shaken, R. asked, "You mean I feel like all girls are like my mom, and the older guys I think they'd like are like my dad?" I confirmed his insight and added that a part of him experienced girls he was attracted to as being *exactly* like his mom and the fellows he imagined they'd prefer as *exactly* like his dad. But that it need not be that way if he could recognize this and begin to sort it out.

R. was soon able to bring himself to ask two girls out on dates. He had several dates with each girl, and decided they were not for him. One told him she "just wanted to be friends," and the other seemed "dumb and giggly" to him. He also completed his first semester of college with C's and D's, and was put on probation for the following semester. Despite his fears (and wishes), he did not flunk out.

Over the summer R. had an appropriate and successful five-day camping trip with two fellows with whom he had been friendly since high school. He proudly told me that he had a good time and "wasn't worried about anything." He also obtained a part-time job, and due to financial pressures on his parents, began to pay for part of his therapy.

Toward the latter part of the summer, R.'s parents and his sister left for a two-week vacation. R.'s brother was working in the area where he attended college, and so R. was home alone. Initially, he was delighted with this freedom, and imagined picking up a girl, taking her home and having intercourse with her. He began attending topless-bottomless bars with several other friends, and was becoming more sexually aroused. He fantasied picking up a girl he had begun to observe regularly as she sat in a park near his home. But then he became worried. Perhaps she had a boyfriend who would find out about his having intercourse with her. He might come to his house with a knife. Maybe he would get "cut up badly" or even killed. I interpreted his fears of being masculine and his expectation that to be sexually masculine resulted, in his mind, in castration or death—in short, awful punishment. I pointed out the triangle that he had again resurrected in this fantasy: a possibly available woman, and her man who will not brook R.'s fooling around with his woman. I interpreted this as his re-experiencing the feelings he had toward his mother when he was a little boy, and his worries about his father's not tolerating his sexual interest in his mother. Soon after this interpretive work, R.'s old symptom, reported by his parents as having occurred during latency, reappeared. He became terrified of "some big, Black, drug-crazed dude" breaking into the house. R. was still home alone at this time. The intruder would break in, R. would wake up, and the robber would stab him to death. R. took to staying awake all night. He saw a Black man near his house one day and worried about this man "casing" the house. Robberies had been reported in his neighborhood, and he was furious at me for not thinking he had good reason to be so frightened. He stayed up until it got light (about 5:30 A.M.), listening for sounds of breaking and entering. It was helpful for R. to have me separate cause to "be concerned" from "feeling panicked." It would be prudent to be sure doors were locked before retiring, and to call the police if someone suspicious were lurking about. But his terror went well beyond being appropriately concerned. Once he could see this distinction, I interpreted his wish to have the intruder come into his bedroom—that was why he wasn't sure whether keeping his radio on would attract or scare off the burglar. When I asked him what "listening for sounds in the night," as he was doing at this time, reminded him of, he recalled being six years old and listening to sounds from his parents' bedroom at night. His bedroom and theirs had a common wall. He would cry and his father would come to comfort him. I pointed out that he felt lonely being all alone in the house now, just as he had felt lonely in his bedroom as a young boy. The sounds he heard then excited him and he had a wish to be with his mother as his dad was—namely in a sexually exciting way. But that was too scary; he imagined his father would be angry and would hurt him for having such thoughts. So instead he wished to be with his father, and in fact his father did come into his bedroom, just as he wished this burglar would. And he was scared this intruder would screw him as he wished his father would. Within two days, his anxiety about a burglar disappeared.

R. is now about to begin his second semester of college in the fall, and has decided to move out of his parents' home and into either a college dormitory or an apartment. Recently he has begun to worry about the amount of "pot smoking" that he has heard occurs in college dormitories. He read a study showing that prolonged use of marijuana results in breast enlargement and he imagines that one's penis would also shrink, since it sounded as if a disruption of hormone functioning was the issue. Although he rarely used marijuana, he had begun to fear that just by being in a dormitory where many people do smoke pot, he would inhale sufficient quantities of smoke to develop breasts and have his penis shrink. I have begun to point out this most recent symptom as yet another expression of his feminine wishes and his anxiety about being turned into a girl via castration. I told him that the opportunities to be successful in a masculine way, by doing well at school and by meeting new girls and dating, must be scaring him a great deal to require him to back away from these exciting possibilities and again begin to feel feminine.

Chapter 6

Comparing Obsessional and Hysterical Personalities

The point is frequently made that the obsessional rearrangement of the structure of the personality leads to a "better," "stronger," "more desirable" personality organization than that made by the hysteric.

This conclusion is partly due to the correct assumption that the development of an obsessional neurosis requires an ego organization of good quality, and partly to the well-known statement by Freud that a "precocious" ego development is among the *predispositions* to the development of an obsessional neurosis.

As mentioned before, certain obsessional character traits are in many ways assets to the personality when present in specific quantities, combinations, and proportions. On the other hand, it is only too well known that other obsessional characters offer combinations of traits of a less desirable nature, which in some cases lead to severe limitations even where a good potential of ego performance exists. What is true of the obsessional character is true in a similar way for neurotic disturbances. According to Ernest Jones (1918) both valuable and disadvantageous qualities derive from "the interrelations of the different anal-erotic components with one another and with other constituents of the whole character." He thinks that among the valuable "may be reckoned especially the individualism, the determination and persistence, the love of order and power of organization, the competency, reliability and thoroughness, the generosity, the bent towards art and good taste, the capacity for unusual tenderness, and the general ability to deal with concrete objects of the material world."

Among the disadvantageous "belong the incapacity for happiness, the irritability and bad temper, the hypochondria, the miserliness, meanness and pettiness, the slow-mindedness and proness to bore, the bent for dictating and tyrannising, and the obstinacy. . . ."

The obsessional neurosis is more severe, more ego-encompassing and crippling than the hysterical neurosis. The prognosis of the former is always more serious than that of the latter for the same reasons. From the point of view of drive organization the obsessional neurosis always implies an important fixation point at the anal-sadistic stage to which an important regressive move has taken place in later development. Here again the hysteric patient's fixation point is at a higher level (the phallic-oedipal) and in this sense compares favorably with the obsessionals.

Nevertheless, and in spite of all that has been said above, clinical observation and experience still points to the special quality of the ego of the obsessional neurotic.

I think that a reconciliation of these apparent contradictions is reached if we state that a minimum "quality" of ego development is required to "produce" an obsessional neurosis, a minimum which is relatively high compared with other forms of psychopathology, including hysterias. This requirement refers even to the most poorly organized forms of obsessional neuroses, let alone the more highly organized ones.

Considering now the hysterical developments from the ego side, there is no doubt that they can start with a lower "quality" than that required for the ego of an obsessional neurosis, provided that their drive organization has proceeded to the appropriate point in its development. But though clinical experience shows that some hysterical disorders occur in otherwise very primitive and poor ego organization, it must be remembered that these are only cases that occur at the lower end and that many other forms of hysterical personality are of the highest order. In short, at the higher end of the scale, hysterics can be as good as, perhaps at times better than, obsessionals from the point of view of the high quality of their ego organization.

It is for the above reason that I think it is a fallacy to assume that the obsessional outcome always implies a better ego or a better personality than the hysterical one.

If we were artificially to express ego quality in grades (grade 1, poor ego development; grade 2, medium ego development; grade 3, good ego development; and grade 4, excellent ego development), then a diagram (Figure 1) would show at one glance that the minimum ego quality required for an obsessional neurosis is grade 3 (good) while the hysterical patient can go down the scale as far as grade 1 (poor).

On the other hand, an obsessional patient with ego development of grade 3 (good) will have a less rich personality, capacity, etc. than the hysterical of the highest order, though it should be clear from the schema that obsessionals can also reach grade 4.

Figure 1

EGO QUALITY

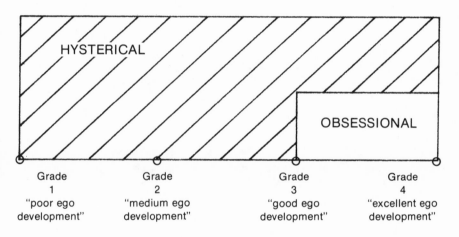

| Grade 1 "poor ego development" | Grade 2 "medium ego development" | Grade 3 "good ego development" | Grade 4 "excellent ego development" |

A similar argument as to the necessary "quality" of ego required applies to other forms of psychopathology. Homosexuals, for example, can like hysterics show a much wider range of variation than can obsessionals as far as the quality of ego organization is concerned; some homosexuals are highly developed while others show a poor ego organization.

I believe that a closer and more detailed study of the ego organization is necessary, as Hartmann (1950) and others have pointed out, to specify what degree of development of what ego functions has been reached, as well as their interaction with the drives and with one another, etc. It is here that many clues are to be found as to the possible outcomes of the developmental and neurotic conflicts of the child. Although *a priori* it looks as if variations are possible ad infinitum, I am inclined to think that certain general and common groupings, combinations and patterns will be discernable.

Chapter 7

A Developmental Approach

When the question of obsessional neurosis is approached developmentally, attention is directed automatically to that particular stage of development where the all-important fixation point is established, i.e., to the anal phase, even though the significance of earlier and later events has to be appreciated also, as will be shown later. (For a fuller account of my views on the significance and interaction of the different developmental phases of childhood and their contribution to the final personality see Nagera, 1966.)

While studying the anal period of development, interest has to be divided equally between the vicissitudes of the child's drive organization, his corresponding ego organization with special regard to the status reached by the various ego functions, and the psychological interaction which is taking place between child and environment. As regards the last named, what is significant is the degree of ego involvement with the objects, i.e., the measure of the child's psychological dependence on the object world. The more precocious the ego development of the child, the more sophistication can be expected in the nature and significance of the object relationships and of the interaction between environment and child. The increased awareness of the environmental demands that accompanies such precocious ego development is, I believe, of special significance in laying down the developmental conditions that will lead to an obsessional outcome at a later stage.

On the other hand, this heightened awareness of environmental attitudes and demands is not the child's only reason for reacting with conflict to the anal-sadistic impulses. Where ego development is precocious the inherent incompatibility between comparatively high aesthetic and moral demands and comparatively low instinctual activity leads to the same result.

In the individual case it is not always easy to determine whether the child's objection to anal sadism have been taken from environmental attitudes, toilet training, etc. or represents an internal ego attitude.

Observation of children going through the anal-sadistic stage of their development shows that even at that early age they tend to react to this situation of conflict with specific symptom formation of a typical obsessional nature, though they cannot be said on this account to suffer from an obsessional neurosis. What has to be established here is whether these early types of symptom formation and ego defense activity are a sure indication of the possible later development of an obsessional neurosis.

In one of the cases studied, the child was described as having been an excessively dirty baby, playing and smearing herself with feces, *but by the time she was two years old* she was very upset when dirty and had to wash her hands a great deal (washing compulsion), thus showing a conflict between what seem to have been strong anal impulses and her ego objections to them at age two. I might mention that in this case and many others one is not really able to determine how exact the mother's description is and furthermore how much collusion there may be between the mother's fantasies and the child's developmental stage. Similarly, it is difficult to judge how severe the environmental reaction may be to the child's anal impulses, especially in cases where the conscious acknowledged attitude of the parents is lenient. We know that the unconscious attitude to the child may be quite different. Nevertheless, important as these considerations are, they do not affect with our present line of argument.

The child in this case came into psychoanalytic treatment at age eleven with one or two quasi-obsessional symptoms though by no means an obsessional neurosis. In fact the bulk of her libido was at the phallic-oedipal stage where her main conflicts were centered. There was a certain amount of regression, with conflict and symptom formation at the oral level where her main fixation point lay, while the anal stage could be shown to play the lesser role in her personality and psychopathology. Even if further regression were to take place in her, these oral fixations would have prevented her from organizing her psychopathology in the form of an obsessional neurosis.

This observation may be considered as typical. There are many children who show a high degree of ego development at the anal-sadistic stage and already, therefore, respond to those impulses by reaction-formations and typical obsessional developments; nevertheless, if they fall ill, they do not develop an obsessional neurosis, but some other form of psychopathology. What they have acquired is no more than a predisposition which may or may not lead to an obsessional development, a point to be discussed later.

Quite frequently this form of defense activity and early symptom formation of an obsessional nature is only transitory, lasting for as long as the anal phase is in the foreground and disappearing with the next developmental move. In this case such symptoms are the expression of a typical developmental conflict, disappearing with the next developmental move if no important fixations are established while going through the phase. (For examples of this type of transitory obsessional-like reaction during the anal phase, see Nagera, 1966, International Universities Press, New York, especially the chapter on developmental conflicts.)

If, on the other hand, an important *fixation point* has been established at the anal stage, this creates another predisposing factor for later obsessional development, although again it will depend on a number of accompanying circumstances whether this path will actually be taken. Such circumstances can be found in the developmental history preceding the anal stage. If fixations have been formed at earlier dates, what is needed is a comparative assessment of the strength of the component instincts of the oral and anal phases, as well as a study of the causes which have led to fixation at the respective levels. Multiple fixations in one and the same personality are a frequent occurrence, and where this is the case the scales have to be weighted clearly on the side of the anal-sadistic stage, to create an obvious predisoposition for obsessional development.

Events after the anal-sadistic stage may prove as decisive as those before in the final integration of the personality. Thus the strength of the phallic-oedipal strivings, the vicissitudes of the phase, and the attitude of the environment to the child's phallic drive have to be considered and compared with the anal organization. If it happens that the phallic-oedipal impulses are even stronger than the anal, they will shift from the anal to the phallic phase the core around which the organization of the personality crystallizes. In that case there may still be an important contribution coming from the anal stage to the structure of the personality, but the essential elements will correspond to the phallic-oedipal phase.

In short, before a final assessment can be made as to the final role to be played by certain factors predisposing to obsessional neurosis, it is necessary to examine not only the anal phase but the previous stage, and to wait for the contribution of the later ones. Such economic considerations as to the contributions of the phases in their own right and in relation to each other are essential to the developmental approach and to developmental thinking.

While many of these considerations deal specifically with the drive organization, there are obviously other factors which explain why regression to an anal fixation point may lead to other than obsessional results to homosexuality, for example, or to one of the sadistic perversions.

To consider further the role of the ego: there are many children who show the usual signs of precocious ego development but who do not seem to raise any noticeable objections to their anality. In certain instances we receive the impression that the anal-sadistic strivings are not of sufficient strength to give rise to significant conflicts or reaction-formations, especially when this quantitative factor is coupled with a comparatively tolerant attitude on the environmental side. It may be of interest here that in at least one of the cases closely observed by me the manifestations of agressive impulses were on the whole well under ego control and offered no particular problem to the child, who was otherwise enterprising and adventurous in tackling all sorts of new situations. This may be a very significant factor in the final outcome. The libidinal and messing aspects were not particularly marked either, but were enjoyed apparently quite freely without the need for control shown in relation to the aggressive impulses.

It may prove important to examine as well the balance between the libidinal and the aggressive components during the anal-sadistic stage. From my observations it seems that they can combine in all sort of proportions, with the emphasis sometimes on the libidinal, sometimes on the aggressive side, or in more or less equal proportions. It is conceivable that when the balance is on the side of the libidinal elements that dominate the picture (because there are in any case some aggressive components always present in the picture), we may tend to generalize from the importance and strength of the former and assume that the latter impulses are of similar strength and importance, when this is indeed not necessarily so. I believe that such a precise discrimination is an important element of judgment to determine which children may possibly develop later into obsessionals, since we do know that strong anal-sadistic *aggressive* elements play such a role in this condition.

On the other hand, children with strong anal-sadistic impulses who exhibit no specific reaction to them during the phase are not necessarily exempt from developing an obsessional neurosis at a later stage. Here, we find the explanation usually in the fact that the degree of ego development during the anal phase is relatively limited and objects to anality are therefore not produced, not even where the environmental attitude towards toilet training is rigid. Such failure to respond to the environmental demand occurs not only where the child's own development is below par but above all where toilet training is started by the parents too early or in too severe a fashion, resulting in a massive "developmental interference" with the child (for examples of such response and definitions of developmental interferences, developmental conflicts, neurotic conflicts, and infantile neurosis, see Nagera, 1966). In such cases it is very probable that an important fixation point will be established at the anal level. At a later date, when further ego progress has been made, if the phallic-oedipal conflicts prove too strong and if regression ensues, the ego's objections to anality will arise belatedly and some form of obsessional development may well be set in motion.

In this connection it may be profitable to define the term "precocious ego" as well as the implications of such precocity for superego formation.

In my usage *precocious ego* implies among other things an early and increased awareness of adult attitudes and of environmental demands in general, in particular in regard to the anal-sadistic impulses. Similarly it implies frequently that a higher level of object relationship than usual for the phase has been reached even at this early stage. This acts as a source of pressure for identification with, and internalization of at least some aspects of the environmental demands, on the basis of the higher psychological dependence on the object.

Thus, in my view, a precocious ego development also tends to imply the early development of important superego precursors and the early establishment of primitive forms of ego ideals. Because of the mechanisms involved in superego formation some aspects of the anal-sadistic impulses are taken into the superego structure and give to it the severe qualities that characterize the superego of obsessionals.

Further, where ego development is precocious and there are present strong ego dystonic anal-sadistic impulses, the processes of internalization take place earlier than in those cases where ego development is not advanced. What happens in the latter case is that the ego development catches up at some late point and then a situation arises somewhat similar to that which existed early on in the case of the precocious ego development. Here the fixations keep the anal-sadistic impulses in the foreground instead of letting them recede into the background. After ego development has caught up, the anal-sadistic impulses have to be faced. The more important and massive the fixation the stronger the anal-sadistic impulses present, and the stronger the objection to them. At some point then, the slowly developing ego may react to whatever anal sadism is present in very much the same way as the precocious one.

We must further consider an important aspect of superego formation in obsessional neurosis. Because of the *regression* from the phallic-oedipal phase that takes place in obsessionals, the final touches to the superego structure that should have been given through the resolution of the Oedipus complex are of a very different nature. Instead of internalizations made on the basis of the fused drive energy of the phallic-oedipal phase and images, the superego structure is further built up on the basis of internalizations of defused drive energy, brought about by the anal-sadistic regression. This partly explains the severe and peculiar nature of the superego structure in obsessional neuroses. It is perhaps what Weissman (1954) had in mind when he said that "in pathological development, the archaically introjected objects are not predominantly replaced by the objects of the mature superego"(he also calls it the "genital superego," seen as largely resulting from the appropriate resolution of the phallic-oedipal phase and from later internalizations). "It is such predominance of an archaic superego," he continued, "that may be of importance in the genesis of obsessional neuroses." In our formulation *archaic* refers not only to early introjections and precursors (in time) but also to those introjects that are acquired quite late in development but that nevertheless, because of their connection with developmentally early and nonfused impulses, will lead to a severe, rigid, sadistic structure, in short to the so-called archaic superego.

Chapter 8

General and Diagnostic
Considerations

It is not uncommon to hear references to the obsessional symptoms that may appear before the oedipal state (that is, during the anal phase) as an obsessional neurosis. Thus, for example, Weissman (1954, p. 538) refers to "preoedipal compulsion neurosis" when discussing some aspects of the treatment by Selma Fraiberg (1952, p. 173) of a two-and-a-half-year-old child with many compulsive symptoms. Similarly, he quotes Hartmann, Kris and Loewenstein's description of *obsessional behavior* in psychotic or retarded children as an attempt to organize a bewildering world that is insufficiently invested with energy, stating then that: "Whether such preoedipal obsessional neurosis has been present in all cases of the more typical postoedipal neurosis has to my knowledge not been studied."

Weissman poses here two interesting questions. One refers to the existence of obsessional neurosis (or for that matter any other form of neurosis proper) before the phallic-oedipal phase has been reached. The second refers to the relationship between what he calls the "preoedipal obsessional neurosis" (whatever one may choose to call these manifestations, the question remains valid) and "the more typical postoedipal [obsessional] neurosis."

In relation to the first, I have already pointed out that the presence of mechanisms of an obsessional type, defenses, and symptoms during the anal phase does not authorize us to speak of an *obsessional neurosis* in the child. As we have seen in a previous chapter, Freud considered an obsessional neurosis the result of a regression to the anal-sadistic stage from the later phallic-oedipal conflicts. To have reached the phallic-oedipal stage is in any case, in the author's opinion, the *sine qua non* of the "infantile neurosis" (the earliest possible "neurosis proper") and all its later varieties. According to these views the phenomena described, of obsessional mechanisms and symptoms during the anal stage, do not yet qualify as an obsessional neurosis; but the question then arises of how to refer to and classify these and similar types of early disturbances and conflicts capable of leading to symptom formation of a very specific nature. I have in another publication (1966) approached this problem, and proposed to classify the early disturbances according to certain characteristics (many of them of a developmental nature) as "developmental interferences," "developmental conflicts," and "neurotic conflicts." I have further tried to distinguish these earlier types of disturbances from the "infantile neurosis" and any of its later variations. I said in the same publication that before we even speak of an infantile neurosis, the phallic-oedipal level of development must have been reached:

This implies that multiple and very complicated maturational developmental processes have had to take place on the side of the drives, on the child's ego and in terms of the capacity for object relationships. Because of this high degree of organization of all aspects of the personality the disturbances taking place against this background can be of a highly complicated nature. The infantile neurosis is in my view an attempt to organize all the previous and perhaps manifold neurotic conflicts and developmental shortcomings, with all the conflicts typical of the phallic-oedipal phase into a single organization, into a single unit of the highest economic significance. This compromise formation is possible at this point because of the relatively high degree of development reached in several areas, particularly on the ego side, especially in its integrative and synthetic function.

The second question posed by Weissman I have tried to answer according to my experience at the Hampstead Clinic (and later on at Children's Psychiatric Hospital, University of Michigan) by saying that there is no direct correlation between preoedipal manifestations of obsessional symptoms and later obsessional developments, and have tried to explain some of the reasons for this (see Chapter 7).

Though, as Freud and others have indicated, obsessional neurosis can develop at any time during latency or adolescence and though the age range studied covers the whole of childhood including adolescence, surprisingly few of the many cases examined in the Hampstead diagnostic department have been diagnosed as obsessional neurosis.

We do see a large number of children where one or another obsessional type of symptom or reaction is or has been present, at some time or another. But they are part of what looks otherwise like mixed neurosis in which the over-all balance (symptomatically and clinically) is certainly not in the direction of obsessional neurosis.

Judging by these observations of children, one would have to conclude that obsessional characters and obsessional neuroses are very rare entities indeed. After several years of observation in a different setting, at the Child Psychoanalytic Study Program at Children's Psychiatric Hospital, and at Children's Psychiatric Hospital itself, I can confirm the statements just made. There is indeed a paucity of well-delineated, clear-cut obsessional neuroses in children and adolescents. Yet clinical experience with adults contradicts this paucity.

The discrepancy is partly accounted for by a developmental tendency to keep conflicts fluid and flexible for as long as possible during childhood. This in part explains why most of the disturbances that we observe in early childhood, latency and even early adolescence, show a diffuse and fluid clinical picture, with conflicts and symptom formation at different levels. The tendency to an early settlement of the situation of conflict in the form of an obsessional neurosis, an obsessional character, or any other form of psychopathology is not only infrequent but viewed with suspicion by the diagnostician and frequently taken to be a doubtful prognostic sign.

Similar to the "quasi" obsessional neurosis developed during the anal-sadistic stage, isolated manifestations of the same type appear also in latency children, even though only a small minority of such cases take the further course into obsessional neurosis. The presence of a few obsessional symptoms within an otherwise florid mixed neurosis at this period does not justify the diagnosis of obsessional neurosis. Weissman (1954) is of the opinion that the frequency of obsessional symptoms in latency is due to the failure of repression and of hysterical symptoms to bind the oedipal conflicts, when on the other hand regression has occurred.

In many such cases observed by the author, the regression to the anal-sadistic fixation point was of a temporary nature and, further, limited in scope, as demonstrated by abundant symptom formation based on the phallic-oedipal conflicts. In this type of case it is essential to assess as closely as possible the relative importance of the various pregenital levels. If a study of the developmental picture of the child does not show a massive fixation at the anal level, and if the usual characteristics pointing to the anal components are missing, we can take it that the obsessional symptoms will be of a transitory nature and that no obsessional neurosis will follow. In this case the obsessional manifestations are no more than the ego's reaction to whatever anality is present in the fluid conflict situation. If, on the other hand, there are clear indications in the history of far-reaching anal fixations, then it is not impossible that the presenting picture of a mixed neurosis will change in due course into obsessional development. The neurosis appears mixed while the conflicts are fought out mostly at the phallic-oedipal level and while regression to anality is limited. The obsessional characteristics move to the fore as soon as the conflict cannot be contained at the higher level and regression proceeds further. (For a fuller account of this and similar problems see Nagera, 1964.) Nunberg has pointed out in his *Principles of Psychoanalysis* (1954, p. 276) that the obsessional neurosis is hardly ever pure and that it frequently begins as a hysteria to be succeeded later, usually in puberty, by the obsessional neurosis.

Several of the cases studied at the Hampstead Clinic showed a completely developed obsessional neurosis sometime between the ages of nine and twelve. This was usually preceded by one or another form of anxiety hysteria with typical phobic symptoms. In some cases the picture of anxiety hysteria had lasted for six or more years until it had finally been replaced by the obsessional neurosis and symptoms. All the cases showed quite clearly at some point in their development the phallic-oedipal conflicts from which a final and massive regression had taken place. Accompanying the phallic-oedipal conflicts there frequently was striking evidence of the intensity of the conflicts around masturbation.

The fact that all these cases had reached the phallic-oedipal stage and the intensity of their conflicts at that level explained why the clinical picture and the mechanisms of symptom formation were very much those of a "hysterical nature." But this was so only as long as the conflicts were fought at the phallic-oedipal level and before regression took place.

In all these cases there was ample evidence, even at the hysterical stage, of the importance of the anal fixation, evidence pointing to the possibility of regression to the anal stage and consequently to the possibility of the later development of an obsessional neurosis. Following are some illustrative cases:

1. F. S. was referred to a child guidance clinic at age eight years, eight months, for a number of phobic symptoms and in particular a phobia for dogs that started at age three. She tested 163 on the Revised Stanford-Binet at age eight and a half, though actually did not give the impression of being that bright. F.'s early ego development is not known in great detail but she walked early and her speech was said to be highly developed by the time she was eleven months. Her toilet training began at birth. She was dry and clean by day at about two years. She was dry at night at about three. By the time she was twelve she was referred to the Hampstead Clinic for treatment. By then she was suffering from an obsessional neurosis with many rituals, compulsive actions, and numerous bedtime ceremonials: the curtain must have a fold in the middle, the chair must be an inch from a given table, the table cloth in the middle of the table, the pillow placed centrally in the bed, the books arranged in a certain order, etc. Unless such arrangements were strictly adhered to, she became extremely anxious and sleep was impossible.

2. Q. S. was a boy of fourteen and a half when referred to the Hampstead Clinic. He had a long history of tics, including the blinking of eyelids since age three and such other tics as head-shaking. They continued until age nine at which time they were partly replaced by an obsession with cleanliness and tidiness. By eleven he was very anxious if books were not replaced in their exact original position and he could not go to bed unless the sheet was tucked in in a particular way, with intense anxiety attacks breaking out when everything was not in order. During the previous eighteen months his obsessions had extended to his clothes, to checking that

every cupboard door was closed, etc. He suffered as well from one or two phobic symptoms, such as a phobia of dogs and of the dark. His I.Q. (Full Scale, WISC): 114.

3. P. S., a girl nine years and eight months old at the time of referral, rated as average to high average as far as intelligence was concerned. This girl experienced great difficulty when school started and suffered from sickness and a fear of leaving home to go to school. From five to seven years there were frequent nightmares which made her go to the parental bedroom, lying in the bed between the father and the mother. Obsessional symptoms started at age eight with compulsive questioning and a number of compulsive actions, and had steadily increased since.

4. O. S. was a girl of twelve and a half when referred to the clinic. Her main symptom was a fear of being sick and compulsive questioning about it. At the same time she had developed a number of rituals and compulsive actions such as knocking her elbows on the table, knocking on the wall six times before picking things up, walking up and down six times before going to bed or dressing herself, etc. At twelve and a half she tested on the Stanford-Binet as high as 156 and the figure was considered a possible underestimate.

It is of diagnostic importance to distinguish between these typically obsessional children and another group of children, ego-defective and backward, who may produce superficially similar symptoms. They are frequently much younger than those referred to above and show what look like obsessional symptoms and certain "ritualistic" pieces of behavior which superficially resemble closely those of the obsessional patients. They want everything done with sameness, in a routine way, and do not tolerate changes. In fact, any departure from the usual procedure, any change of routine, tends to produce severe anxiety. For example, they want to sit in the same place at the dining table, at approximately the same time, and will use only the same glass, dishes and other familiar utensils. If this is not complied with they are thrown into an acute anxiety state. This behavior to the casual observer closely resembles the truly obsessional need to keep exactly to the prescribed routine of ritualistic behavior or otherwise face large amounts of anxiety. Nevertheless a careful examination will show the completely different nature of the two groups of manifestations. In the latter group of children the need for uniformity and routine is due to the limited capacity of their ego to grasp and cope with even the slightest change. Any alteration in familiar routine makes it impossible for their damaged egos to cope with the "new" situation. Thus, they react with massive anxiety.

The differential diagnosis with a true obsessional development is generally not difficult to appreciate, since the ego defects and general backwardness of these latter children are quite ostensible and soon clear away any doubts. The following is an illustration of this type of case:

5. Z. V. was referred to the Hampstead Clinic at age seven and reported to have been very backward ever since she was a year old. She could not feed herself until two and a half; she refused to drink except from a spoon until the age of three, taking neither bottle nor cup once she was weaned. Speech was delayed. At about four and a half she was able to repeat words parrotlike and started on a few sentences, expressing only her immediate wants. She walked in reasonably good time. At five years, nine months, the test result (Binet-Simon Scale) showed an I.Q. of about 52. Different observers referred to her having many "obsessional habits." The mother explained that Z. took changes badly and clung to certain habits and clothes, that it was very difficult to get her to change into winter or summer clothes, that she always had to have a jacket on, etc. The father explained that her whole life consisted of routine, and nothing but routine. In putting on her dressing gown, turning on the lights and drawing the curtains, there was a certain sequence which had to be followed to avoid the child's being upset.

References

Abraham, K. (1912). A complicated ceremonial found in neurotic women. *Selected Papers on Psycho-Analysis.* London: The Hogarth Press.

———(1919). A particular form of neurotic resistance against the psycho-analytic method. *Selected Papers on Psycho-Analysis.* London: The Hogarth Press.

———(1921). Contributions to the theory of the anal character. *Selected Papers on Psycho-Analysis.* London: The Hogarth Press.

———(1921). A short study of the development of the libido viewed in the light of mental disorders. *Selected Papers on Psycho-Analysis.* London: The Hogarth Press.

Alexander, F. (1948). *Fundamentals of Psychoanalysis.* New York: W. W. Norton.

Barnett, J. (1966). On cognitive disorders in the obsessional. *Contemporary Psychoanalysis* 2: 122-134.

———(1969). On aggression in the obsessional neuroses. *Contemporary Psycho-Analysis* 6: 48-57.

Blacker, K. H. (1966). Obsessive-compulsive phenomena and catatonic states: a continuum. *Psychiatry* 29: 185-194.

Bonnard, A. (1950). The mother as therapist in a case of obsessional neurosis. *Psychoanalytic Study of the Child* 5: 391-408.

Bornstein, B. (1953). Fragment of an analysis of an obsessional child. *Psychoanalytic Study of the Child* 8: 313-332.

Brunswick, R. M. (1950). A supplement to Freud's History of an infantile neurosis. *The Psychoanalytic Reader.* London: The Hogarth Press and the London Institute of Psychoanalysis.

Bychowski, G. (1966). Obsessive-compulsive facade in schizophrenia.

International Journal of Psycho-Analysis 47: 189-198.

Chethik, M. (1969). The therapy of an obsessive-compulsive boy, some treatment considerations. *Journal of the American Academy of Child Psychiatry* 8: 465-484.

Fenichel, O. (1945). *The Psycho-Analytic Theory of Neurosis.* New York: W. W. Norton.

Ferenczi, S. (1913). Stages in the development of the sense of reality. *Contributions to Psycho-Analysis.* New York: Dover.

Fraiberg, S. (1952). A critical neurosis in a two-and-a-half-year-old girl. *Psychoanalytic Study of the Child* 7: 173-215.

Freud, A. (1937). *The Ego and the Mechanisms of Defence.* London: The Hogarth Press and the London Institute of Psychoanalysis.

———(1965). *Normality and Pathology in Childhood, Assessment of Development.* New York: International Universities Press.

———(1962). Assessment of childhood disturbances. *Psychoanalytic Study of the Child* 17: 149-158.

———(1966). Obsessional neurosis: a summary of psycho-analytic views as presented at the congress. *International Journal of Psycho-Analysis* 47: 116-123.

———, Nagera, H., and Freud, E. (1965). Metapsychological assessment of the adult personality: the adult profile. *Psychoanalytic Study of the Child* 20: 9-41.

Freud, S. (1894a). The neuro-psychoses of defence. *Standard Edition* 3: 39-70.

———(1896a). Heredity and the etiology of the neuroses. *Standard Edition* 3: 141-158.

———(1896b). Further remarks on the neuro-psychoses of defence. *Standard Edition* 3: 162-189.

———(1907b). Obsessive actions and religious practices. *Standard Edition* 9: 115-128.

———(1908b). Character and anal erotism. *Standard Edition* 9: 167-176.

———(1909d). Notes upon a case of obsessional neurosis. *Standard Edition* 10: 153-318.

———(1912x). Totem and taboo. *Standard Edition* 13: 1-164.

———(1913i). The disposition to obsessional neurosis. *Standard Edition* 12: 311-326.

———(1914g). Remembering, repeating and working through. *Standard Edition* 12: 145-156.

———(1915d). Repression. *Standard Edition* 14: 141-158.

———(1915e). The Unconscious. *Standard Edition* 14: 159-218.

———(1916x). Introductory lectures on psycho-analysis. *Standard Edition* 15-16.

————(1917c). On transformations of instinct as exemplified in anal erotism. *Standard Edition* 17: 125-134.

————(1923a). Two encyclopedia articles. *Standard Edition* 18: 255-262.

————(1923b). The Ego and the id. *Standard Edition* 19: 3-68.

————(1926d). Inhibitions, symptoms and anxiety. *Standard Edition* 20: 77-123.

————(1939a). Moses and monotheism. *Standard Edition* 23: 3-140.

————(1950a). *Letters to Fliess,* No. 79.

Gabe, S. (1965). The genetic determinants of obsessive-compulsive phenomena in character formation: a report on a panel of the American Psychoanalytic Association. *Journal of the American Psychoanalytic Association* 13: 591-605.

Gelfman, M. (1970). The role of responsibility in obsessive-compulsive neurosis. *Contemporary Psycho-Analysis* 7: 36-47.

Gero, G., and Rubinfine, D. L. (1955). On obsessive thoughts. *Journal of the American Psychoanalytic Association* 3: 222-243.

Glover, E. (1936). A developmental study of the obsessional neuroses. *International Journal of Psycho-Analysis* 16: 131-144.

————(1955). *The Technique of Psycho-Analysis.* London: Bailliere, Tindall and Cox. *See also Psychoanalysis.* Staples Press, 1939.

Greenacre, P. (1922-23). A study of the mechanism of obsessive-compulsive conditions. *American Journal of Psychiatry* 2: 527-538.

Greenson, R. R. (1966). Comment on Dr. Ritvo's paper. *International Journal of Psycho-Analysis* 47: 149-151.

Grinberg, L. (1966). The relationship between obsessive mechanisms and a state of self-disturbance: depersonalization. *International Journal of Psycho-Analysis* 47: 177-184.

Grunberger, B. (1966). Some reflections on the rat-man. *International Journal of Psycho-Analysis* 47: 160-169.

Hartmann, H. (1933). An experimental contribution to the psychology of obsessive-compulsive neurosis—on remembering completed and uncompleted tasks. *Essays on Ego Psychology.* London: The Hogarth Press and The London Institute of Psychoanalysis, 1964.

————(1950). Psychoanalysis and developmental psychology. *Essays on Ego Psychology.* London: The Hogarth Press and The London Institute of Psycho-Analysis, 1964.

Hoffer, W. (1955). *Psychoanalysis, Practical and Research Aspects.* Baltimore: Williams and Wilkins.

Jones, E. (1913). Hate and anal erotism in the obsessional neurosis. *Papers on Psychoanalysis.* 2nd ed. Baltimore: Williams and Wilkins, 1918.

————(1918). Anal-erotic character traits. *Papers on Psychoanalysis.* London: Bailliere, Tindall and Cox, 1948.

————(1923). Hate and anal erotism in the obsessional neurosis. *Papers on Psychoanalysis.* 2nd and 3rd eds. London: Bailliere, Tindall and Cox.

————(1952). *Sigmund Freud, Life and Work.* Vol. 2. London: The Hogarth Press.

Joseph, B. (1966). Persecutory anxiety in a four-year-old boy. *International Journal of Psycho-Analysis* 47: 184-189.

Kayton, L., and Borge, G. F. (1967). Birth order and the obsessive-compulsive character. *Archives of General Psychiatry* 17: 751-754.

Kestenberg, J. S. (1966). Rhythm and organization in obsessive-compulsive development. *International Journal of Psycho-Analysis* 47: 151-160.

Klein M. (1927). Criminal tendencies in normal children. *Contributions to Psycho-Analysis.* London: The Hogarth Press, 1948.

————(1931). A contribution to the theory of intellectual inhibition. *Contributions to Psycho-Analysis.* London: The Hogarth Press, 1948.

————(1932). *The Psycho-Analysis of Children.* London: The Hogarth Press and The London Institute of Psychoanalysis, 1963.

————(1940). Mourning and its relation to manic-depressive states. *Contributions to Psycho-Analysis.* London: The Hogarth Press, 1948.

————(1946). Notes on some schizoid mechanisms. *Developments in Psycho-Analysis.* London: The Hogarth Press and The London Institute of Psychoanalysis, 1952.

————(1952). Some theoretical conclusions regarding the emotional life of the infant. *Developments in Psycho-Analysis.* London: The Hogarth Press and The London Institute of Psychoanalysis, 1952.

Kline, P. (1967). Obsessional traits and emotional instability in a normal population. *British Journal of Medical Psychology* 40: 153-157.

————(1968). Obsessional traits, obsessional symptoms and anal erotism. *British Journal of Medical Psychology* 43: 293-305.

Kringlen, E. (1970). Natural history of obsessional neurosis. *Seminars in Psychiatry* 2: 403-419.

Laufer, M. (1965). Assessment of adolescent disturbances: the application of Anna Freud's diagnostic profile. *Psychoanalytic Study of the Child* 20:

Lewin, B. (1948). Obsessional neuroses. *Psycho-Analysis Today.* Ed. Sandor Lorand. London: George Allen and Unwin.

Loewenstein, R. M. (1945). A special form of self-punishment. *Psycho-Analytic Quarterly* 14: 46-61.

Lorand, S. (1947). Compulsion neurosis. *The Year Book of Psychoanalysis* 3: 129-140. New York: International Universities Press.

Michaels, J., and Porter, R. T. (1949). Psychiatric and social implications of contrasts between psychopathic personality and obsessive compulsion neurosis. *The Journal of Nervous and Mental Disease* 109: 122-132.

Morgenthaler, F. (1966). Psychodynamic aspects of defence with comments on technique in the treatment of obsessional neuroses. *International Journal of Psycho-Analysis* 47: 203-209.

Nacht, S. (1966). The interrelationship of phobia and obsessional neurosis. *International Journal of Psycho-Analysis* 47: 136-139.

Nagera, H. (1963). The developmental profile: some considerations regarding its clinical applications. *Psychoanalytic Study of the Child* 18: 511-541.

———(1964). On arrest in development, fixation and regression. *Psycho-Analytic Study of the Child* 19: 222-240.

———(1966). *Early Childhood Disturbances, the Infantile Neurosis and the Adulthood Disturbances: Problems of a Developmental Psychoanalytic Psychology.* New York: International Universities Press. Monograph No. 2 of *Psychoanalytic Study of the Child.*

Nunberg, H. (1955). *Principles of Psychoanalysis.* New York: International Universities Press.

Parker, B. (1965). The role of a specific father-child interaction pattern in the genesis and psychoanalytic treatment of obsessional character neurosis. *International Journal of Psycho-Analysis* 46: 332-342.

Pearson, G. (1940). A case of compulsive neurosis in an eleven-year-old-boy. *American Journal of Orthopsychiatry* 10: 136-151.

Pious, W. L. (1950). Obsessive-compulsive in an incipient schizophrenic. *Psychoanalytic Quarterly* 19: 327-351.

Ramzy, I. (1966). Factors and features of early compulsive formation. *International Journal of Psycho-Analysis* 47: 169-177.

Reich, W. (1928). On character analysis. *The Psychoanalytic Reader.* London: The Hogarth Press and the London Institute of Psychoanalysis, 1950.

Rice, E. (1974). The compulsive companion: a case study. *International Journal of Psychoanalytic Psychotherapy* 3: 48-72.

Ritvo, S. (1966). Correlations of a childhood and adult neuroses: based on the adult analysis of a reported child case. *International Journal of Psycho-Analysis* 47: 130-132.

Robinson, L. H. (1974). Sleep and dreams in the analytic hour: the analysis of an obsessional patient. *Psychoanalytic Review* 61: 115-131.

Rosen, V. H. (1966). Comment on Dr. Morgenthaler's paper. *International Journal of Psycho-Analysis* 47: 210-212.

Rosenberg, C. M. (1967). Personality and obsessional neurosis. *British Journal of Psychiatry* 113: 471-477.

Sachs, H. (1947). The transformations of impulses into the obsessional ritual. *The Year Book of Psychoanalysis* 3: 141-147. New York: International Universities Press.

Salzman, L. (1965). Obsessions and phobias. *Contemporary Psycho-Analysis* 2: 1-25.

Sandler, J. and Hazari, A. (1960). The "obsessional": on the psychological classification of obsessional character traits and symptoms. *British Journal of Medical Psychology* 33: 113-122.

Sandler, J. and Jaffe, W. G. (1965). Notes on obsessional manifestations in children. *Psychoanalytic Study of the Child* 20: 425-441.

Schilder, P. (1940). The structure of obsessions and compulsions. *Psychiatry* 3: 549-560. *See also* The organic background of obsessions and compulsions. *American Journal of Psychiatry*, 1938.

Sifneos, P. E. (1966). Psychoanalytically oriented short-term dynamic or anxiety-producing psychotherapy for mild obsessional neuroses. *Psychiatric Quarterly* 40: 270-282.

Sterba, R. (1942). *Introduction to the Psychoanalytic Theory of the Libido.* New York: Nervous and Mental Disease Monographs, 1947.

van der Leeuw, J. (1966). Comment on Dr. Ritvo's paper. *International Journal of Psycho-Analysis* 47: 132-135.

Weissman, P. (1954). Ego and superego in obsessional character and neurosis. *Psychoanalytic Quarterly* 23: 529-543.

———(1956). On pregenital compulsion phenomena and the repetition compulsion. *Journal of the American Psychoanalytic Association* 4: 503-510.

Wexler, M. (1966). Comment on Dr. Bychowski's paper. *International Journal of Psycho-Analysis* 47: 198-203.

Winnicott, D. W. (1966). Comment on obsessional neurosis and "Frankie". *International Journal of Psycho-Analysis* 47: 143-145.

Wisdom, J. O. (1964). A methodological approach to the problem of obsessional neurosis. *British Journal of Medical Psychology* 37: 145-159.

Wulff, M. (1951). The problem of neurotic manifestations in children of preoedipal age. *Psychoanalytic Study of the Child* 6: 169-179.

Index